Gertie's
Dream Garden

GAIL LOGAN

iUniverse®

GERTIE'S DREAM GARDEN

iUniverse books may be ordered through booksellers or by contacting:

iUniverse
1663 Liberty Drive
Bloomington, IN 47403
www.iuniverse.com
1-800-Authors (1-800-288-4677)

ISBN: 978-1-5320-7648-0 (sc)
ISBN: 978-1-5320-7649-7 (e)

Library of Congress Control Number: 2019907547

Print information available on the last page.

iUniverse rev. date: 07/18/2019

"One touch of nature makes the whole world kin."
—William Shakespeare

This book's sketches and above photo are by Gail Logan.

"Much has been written about the polar rounds but very little has been said about the corresponding shift of the equator .Certainly climatic changes in the temperate and tropical zones have caused many more migrations and led to the destruction of many more civilizations than any changes in polar regions."

Mathematician, Apollo 11 Space Scientist,
and author, Maurice Chatelain

GERTIE'S GARDEN

Gertie the garden spider may seem a bit long legged and scary.
For those who know her well though, she is quite the contrary.
Given a chance to make friends, Gertie will win you over again and again.

Sometimes she'll hang out in an unkempt garden where she'll spin a fine
silken web between an old wooden fence and a tree that is quite dead.

Gertie knows she's big and easily seen so she chooses to bask in the sun
where her bright yellow body matches the colors of sunflowers or yellow
leaves. Her long black legs are lean and strong. Gertie is known to pull
herself up to heights where some might say she doesn't belong.

Gertie often settles comfortably upon a sunflower bloom as birds above
look around for her and become quite confused. Her camouflaged coloring
blends so well with her surroundings that birds who find her kind to be a
delicious snack can't find Gertie or make an attack.

Gertie is content to be left alone. She'll wait for hours or even days so she
may home in on a beetle that is quite alone. Although Gertie isn't cruel,
she has to eat. The unsuspecting beetle soon will become treats. Gertie is
grateful to the beetle for being so good about his defeat.

She spins a silken thread tightly about his brown shiny body but only until
after she's stung him quietly and the beetle has become immoveable and
quite groggy. Gertie then checks her egg sacs nearby. The sacs are safe and
dry. She is relieved to know her babies will survive.

Now that summer days are waning, Gertie must leave her garden nest and
find an appropriate place to rest. Fall is just around the corner, and the
late summer nights are beginning to get colder.

Gertie moves more slowly each succeeding day. Her black and yellow legs are getting rather gray. She stops to rest upon a late Gardenia bloom. Her body feels heavy and tired too. She crawls towards a hole hidden behind a house shingle. Gertie knows she may rest there. She'll wait for Nature to mend what needs to be repaired but before she succumbs to sleep, she'll peek from the shingle hole and gaze at her egg sacs once more. She is pleased her children will have meat for she is leaving her beetle legacy behind. Yet Gertie wants to stay even if it's just for one more day. The early fall morning is crisp and bright. The beautiful blue sky enveloping the world is a wondrous sight. The bright light surrounding her is making everything around her a sheer delight.

Gertie wants to continue gazing at everything today even if it is just halfway. When she has the strength, Gertie again will sit on the sunflower's head and admire the beauty surrounding her.

She'll look out and see all the things she loves the best: A carefree deer meandering freely, the baby squirrels playing in the trees, the green lizard slithering from leaf to leaf or a butterfly sipping nectar from a flowering tree.

Gertie is getting tired. She moves back to her hole behind the house shingle. Her beautiful yellow and black body now is safely hidden. She knows that life will go on while she is asleep, that everything around her is growing and changing. She is glad to have had so many wonderful days. Gertie will wait for a few more hours to pass, and then she will look at a new summer day as if she were gazing in a glass.

Gail Logan

GERTIE'S DREAM

Gertie the garden spider has slipped away:
Behind an old loose shingle she sleeps today.
She dreams of life's greenery and all things
Living freely:
The mourning dove's soft cooing, the amaryllis
blooming,
Are a part of life's reverie that Gertie beholds amidst
Fall's hues of yellow, red and gold.
She is determined she won't forget anything bright this
Sunny day so she listens to feathers rustling in the wind
Or beholds a praying mantis' stance against a world.
of sin.
Wild butterflies landing on flowers
Are part of Gertie's dreamy web like bower.
She spins a web fine, and is determined that none of the
things she knew
She ever will leave behind.
She catches each day's wonder in her web,
And hangs those precious images by her silky bed.

Gail Logan

ABELEY

When dawn came to Abeley, a village by the sea,
A stranger came to Abeley to rendezvous with me.
He smiled from the distance, then stood before me
In the sand.
His eyes were dark and penetrating, he came and
Kissed my hand.
What is it like where you will take me?
He turned, and looked away."It is a place where
The wind blows, where the sea and sky are gray. No
ship sails there
except for mine for no map will chart the way."
I wept at the thought of leaving as we set sail with the
tide.
I watched the land fade into obscurity and the sun
sink beneath the sky.
It seemed like an eternity before I realized,
I was part of infinity, unable to touch mortal hand.
I was immortal never to set foot on land
but destined to sail forever on an uncharted sea
With the stranger who stood beside me,
The stranger from Abeley.

Gail Logan

For years my family kept a home in Wellfleet, Cape Cod which was then a small town for artists and those who wanted to partake of the enormous beauty of a desolate rather lonely place overlooking sea and quiet harbor.

We lived in a home surrounded by protective pines and brush but we were situated not far from a cove where all sorts of wild land and sea birds and other small animals lived. The cove opened into the bay and, across the bay was the charming unspoiled town of Wellfleet, where we knew most of the residents living in town in this quiet little community that dated back to the 17th C. The echoes of the past were apparent in many ways, for remains of ancient native Indian settlements had been found on Indian Neck Rd not far from where we lived.

Less than five or six miles from Wellfleet, was the open sea, the magnificent N. Atlantic Ocean, or the back shore as lower Cape Cod residents from Orleans, Eastham Wellfleet or Truro liked to call it. During winter, so many years ago, few Wellfleet residents spent much time near the back shore but practically everyone kept busy during winter months, and much of the leisure activity, during those months, after the few summer visitors had left, revolved around the local churches, the Saturday night movie or a few community activities such as crafts or bake sales. Although I had friends my own age living in town with their parents I often found myself alone during winter months so I would ride my bike down the end of Cove Rd where it converged with Pilgrim Springs Rd. to the left and Indian Neck Beach road to the right. I always peddled my bike to Indian Neck Rd. beach, which overlooks Black Fish Creek near where "Pilgrim Springs", at low tide bubbles up. As I continued on my way, I would listen to the wind whistling in the telephone wires that lined Indian Neck Rd. There was something ghostly about that place during those dark winter days. I could feel the legacy of a past surround me as it did too on the walks with my family in early spring or fall along Great Island across the bay from where we lived or at the back shore of the N. Atlanta where there was so much light and beauty on beaches teeming with birds and wild life

6

that hid in reeds along the beach or nestled in the woodland ponds behind dunes where toads, frogs and turtles depended on fresh water for survival.

On clear fall days, after sitting with my parents on the beach at the back shore where we enjoyed a picnic lunch, I would climb the great dune behind us and gaze out to sea. Despite all the beauty, I couldn't help but think of the bones of wrecked ships partially buried in sand along the beach. And one wreck in particular would haunt me. When you are alone on a beach like this one, you feel things. The wreck of the pirate ship, Whydah off Wellfleet's back shore in 1717 wasn't yet fully recovered, but that wreck and others that were recovered are tragedies that unconsciously found their way into my poetry: Was Samuel Bellamy on his way to Eastham to fetch his beloved when he disappeared? Legend says he was. If you peruse certain of my poems, "The Love Within", "The Diary of a White Witch", "The Shadow" or "Abeley", you'll realize how a place of great beauty and desolation such as Wellfleet can inspire the imagination.

Truth sometimes is shrouded in mystery especially if there is gold or money involved. Some records indicate that pirate Samuel Bellamy survived the wreck of the Whydah, April 26, 1717.
He wasn't among the 102 bodies that washed ashore on a Wellfleet beach nor was he among the 40 who went missing after the wreck or the nine survivors, six of whom were hanged for piracy in Boston in Oct, 1717 (King George I pardon of all pirates arrived three weeks too late). Those numbers included those aboard his other ship, The Mary Ann that wrecked the same day as the Whydah did. In fact, Bellamy was seen alive and well dressed but not in good health in Wellfleet/Eastham in 1720. If he knew how to find his beloved he never found her. Instead, he kept returning to the place where they had met but Maria Hallet wasn't there. Some say she was a married woman, estranged from her husband when Bellamy met her but that rumor remains unsubstantiated. She and Bellamy had a child but he died. He promised to take her to the West Indies where they would have a new life together. In fact, there probably could be no other reason for Bellamy to return to Wellfleet and Eastham that fateful day if that hadn't been the plan. Had she betrayed him in some way? A dying survivor of the

Whydah told her where to find treasure and she found it. She never found Bellamy though. She walked the dunes and beaches looking for him in vain. When he died, his body was found in the apple orchard where he met her then carried to a tavern for later burial but where? Was his body taken to the burying acre near the apple orchard? Little is known about Samuel Bellamy or where he was laid to rest. One thing is known though, Maria Hallett, the beautiful white witch reputedly committed suicide a week after her lover's death, yet her burial place remains unknown too.

Gail Logan

LADY ARACHNE (GERTIE'S NOBLE FRIEND)

Like an acrobat hanging from a thread,
Lady Arachne weaves her silken web.
Once defeated and shunned,
Pushed aside for her valor,
This spider has survived without guile.
Diminished yet unconquered and skilled,
She has made Minerva, a goddess withdraw
From a challenge unfulfilled.
Mistakenly mishapened, yet nimble though slight,
The beautiful Arachne has turned from the fight.
With assurance and power she pulls herself upward.
She turns daring somersaults, then freefalls without fright.
She climbs even higher then disappears in the light.

Gail Logan

THE FALLEN

At dawn, when sky was fiery red, a golden rooster cried for a world that
bled.
For the fallen one, the Sun god's son's burning descent from sky,
Left countless cities destroyed and in decline.
Today the forest where the sacred deer roamed, and man and
Beast once lived side by side beneath the brilliant sky is gone.
Instead gray somber smoke penetrates a changed world,
Where weeping forest nymphs surround the sacred deer, his hide pierced
by his beloved
Cyparissus' misdirected arrow.
The ruddy ground and the deer's noble jeweled antlered head
Where birds once found refuge is broken and still, and
Cyparissus mourns in torment and self pity for his careless cruel act.
He begs the gods to let him die beside the deer's lifeless side.
He cries too for the blackened forest landscape.
The youth's anguished appeal to the gods and death wish is profound,
Its roots deep and the handsome Cyparissus finally is pitied.
In his place, amidst the charred forest all around,
Grows the Cypress tree, the symbol of Cyparissus' grief for a fallen world,
and the fiery descent of the one who brought death to the world.

Gail Logan

THE SUN GOD MOURNS

The Sun god in darkness mourned his son Phaeton's fiery fall from sky.
He turned his lamp away from Earth,
As if the world never again would know warmth and mirth.
Yet light once more would touch Earth serenely where the sun god's
Horses wandered freely imbibing ambrosia along
The sacred path where the Sun god's beloved Leucothoe,
More beautiful even than his immortal mother Eurynome,
Basked in the golden godly presence.
No being, mortal or divine was dearer
To the Sun god or knew love more sublime.
Not even Clytie or any of the god's former lovers, were treated
With such favor by him. Yet soon the heavenly ray that casts light
On all living things would dim.
Clouds of grief
would engulf him. A shadow would cross
The Sun god's heart when beloved Leucothoe was discovered buried
Beneath earth where the Sun's bright rays couldn't mend the deadly curse
dealt
By Clytie's cruel blow. Left to mourn in a blaze of passionate grief,
The Sun god watched Leucothoe become at one with earth
Until a bush bearing sweet frankincense, a symbol of a god's beloved who
had been,
Grew to quench the insatiable grief of a god who mourns within

Gail Logan

ECHO AND NARCISSUS

Beautiful Echo has only one fear.
She finds herself immortal within her realm
Where eternal years may pass,
And Nature's image of love appears
Only in a glass.
She calls to Narcissus but he doesn't seem to hear.
Absorbed in self, he sees only his own image in waters clear.
Ready to die for that love, he'd rather be engulfed
By depths of cold disdain than be embraced by
Echo's lovely frame.
"Come to me", she cries and rents her hair in vain.
Only her voice returns to her without love's claim.
"Drown in your tears", murmurs a careless Narcissus,
Who slips and falls at river's edge.
He reaches out a desperate arm to Echo near
Bur this time she's speechless and lets Narcissus
Go without a tear.

Gail Logan

THE FAIRY GARDEN

My garden holds a secret dear, a fairy child's retreat.
I am that fairy child again with daisies at my feet
I wander back in time to a place I long to be.
I sit beneath a willow tree with no one there but me.
I listen to the music of a nearby babbling brook.
I watch a wandering butterfly within my shady nook.
The treasures here within this realm are dear and very rare.
A life to live and truly share is here without a care.
Although the childhood days are gone, I do remember well.
The fairy child within still lives and now alone will tell.
The purple lilac's fragrance of garden snails and shells,
Are images of yesterday,
Of things I love so well.
The soulful sounds of Nature must never be swept away for there
Within that music, the fairy child plays.
She sings of distant summers, of flowers that are real.
She plays a lonesome fiddle with crickets in the field.
The fairy child listens. She hears her golden self.
The distant voice of laughter is answered by an elf.
A leaping frog, a babbling brook, restore the weary self.
It's time to leave my fairy world: it's done with aching heart.
I vow to soon return again and nevermore depart.

Gail Logan

THE PERFECT GARDEN

This perfect garden of old is a place without decay;
A world devoid of sonar harpoons or oil ridden waters,
A place where no sign says,
"Come back tomorrow."
The garden gate is open wide.
Why don't we go forward and step inside?
Instead we hesitate and wait as if
Nature had made a mistake.
Nature's plan needn't be abandoned or delayed
As if Creation was the cause of dismay.
We must listen to Earth's steady beat and not
Push aside seasons as if they were cause for defeat.
No alterations are needed in this natural world sublime.
Earth's creation works in perfect time.
Who are we that we should stand without a plan
Tearing everything apart on this grand land?
Hasn't it been said and with praise,
"He saw what he had made and behold it was good?"
That statement must apply to lab mice too and all
Else that we view.

Gail Logan

GAIL

MESSAGE FROM A
FERAL FRIEND

She was a shadow on the ground,
A half hidden figure sleeping in a tree.
She was a wild vine covered feline peering
At the faraway and unseen.
Was she a small panther or beast of prey?
Had she come for just a day?
I knew she couldn't remain.
Yet this visitor from a distant past did stay.
Her green piercing eyes spoke as no words can convey.
Feral and true to Earth, she lingered close whenever
Turbulent winds blew and rains beat upon earth.
Finally when spring rains ceased,
And winds stopped blowing,
She disappeared along a hidden trail
Toward a place I couldn't trace.
Then half dreaming, I heard her as if she spoke words.
"When your life boat drifts towards land on an unseen sea,
Someday you and I will meet and again be free."

Gail Logan

REMA

My little black kitty ran away
Or perhaps she went a different way today.
On Halloween night, I kept her from her usual
Evening flight,
And her friend, Owl missed their camaraderie
For the two made a pact to join one another.
Whether it was in darkness or beneath a moonlight blanket,
They made their way each night
Over sweet smelling fields and forests bright.
But perhaps this time they came upon
A sight so enticing that they decided not to end the flight.
Oh my dear little black kitty has run away.
How can one bear such a thought today?
I gaze out the window on early morns,
And hope I'll find my kitty making her way towards my door.

Gail Logan

REAMA

Reama rests in the shade of a dogwood tree,
And gazes mysteriously through the leaves.
Her dark feline form, her lovely green eyes display
Such concentration,
One wonders what she must contrive.
So still is she, like some ancient statue.
Is she a prop for the day's play of action?
She seems as if she's come to seize an ignominious mouse so
Determined is she that the creature won't enter my house.
Yet Reama's stance is more than that of protector of domain.
A goddess by descent,
She knows her place within life's intent,
Is that of enchantress and creature of night.
How dare the owl ignore her when he takes his evening flight!
The world she is looking for is just out of sight.
Over the hill, to the right of the creek:
They both are familiar, this owl and feline, with a place unknown to men,
A place they can design and amend.
He's come to protect her, this huge bird of prey.
The two must make haste and be on their way.
Tonight the owl hovers gently above her.

As they pull back a veil and enter a dale where
Toads, elves and fairies prevail,
They witness the dark of the moon.
They take part in a ritual men never may see but only assume.

For awhile at least Nature rules the earth.
How dare men tread on such sacred turf!

They savor wild freedom, a kingdom set apart,
Until the night is over and they must depart.
"Oh dear", muses Reama returning to her place in the tree.
"When will men truly love us by recognizing Nature's world to a fuller
degree?"

Gail Logan

THE HEART'S DIARY,

She is my heart box, my diary of dreams.
Whenever I open that box, she always is there it seems.
As sweet as a chocolate candy, and warm as the morning sun,
Cookie was there when I needed her especially when life wasn't fun.
Her black coat, white tipped tail and paws, enhanced her beauty.
Cookie had no flaws.
I remember the first time I lost her. She really hadn't run away.
I hugged her as with tail wagging, she rose up to greet me that day.
Years later, when she finally left me that clear
November night, losing her was like a cruel
wind cutting through my life.
Often I think of Cookie along with other beloved dogs I've known.
One never should say that animals have no souls.
To love a dog like Cookie is to realize that losing one
Means losing part of something that makes you whole

Gail Logan

A HIDDEN PLACE

This hidden place of long ago
Where fiddler crabs scurry into holes,
And whales bask lazily in warm summer sun
Is a realm devoid of the
Pain and violence of a man made domain.
This hidden place is a journey, a peaceful quest
Along endless beaches where the sound of rolling surf,
Like some tempestuous mighty watery chain,
Breaks and keeps pace
With Creation's unending perfect refrain.

Gail Logan

THE MOURNING DOVE

Your name conveys the meaning of what you are.
You defy time's barriers when from afar
Your haunting coo's lamenting cry travels infinitely upward,
And penetrates early morning sky.
Last year you came not to the feeder here
But instead to gaze at your soul mate's
Image in the garden pool clear.
Today I weep to see your humble gray feathery form
Dead, asleep upon winter's icy bed.
Cold wind envelopes you in its weary frill.
I pick you up with my warm hands
As if to awaken you from winter's plan.
Your wing is grazed but not your heart.
Your song is heard again and will not depart.
Your spirit lingers as soulfully you cry
For a love that lives never to die.

Gail Logan

ODE TO A PIGEON

The pigeon plays a useful role in cleaning up life's messes.
The food folks drop in the parking lot can feed an entire feathery flock
On almost any city block.
Our pigeon pal is no gourmet. The food just gets swept away.
He's grateful for any morsel small.
He's dignified too. Pigeon defends his territory as if it were his all,
And not just a place to gorge on lunch away from pests.
Squirrels, Pigeon will remind, you are at times an unruly bunch.
Yes dining with a pigeon is a habit to consider
While sitting on a park bench without a care or jitter:
Until an unlikely blob falls upon one's vest or dress and one has a mess.
As for the pigeon, he flies away as if he never meant to stay.
Ah, one mustn't be upset. There's always the cleaners. No need to fret.
Pigeons are just birds, not the fancy kind either.
They're no good for eating at Thanksgiving dinner.
And for birdwatchers intent on seeing gorgeous feathers,
These gray plucky fellows are mere poster birds for Audubon nevers.
Yet if I went bird watching, I'd have my d'ruthers.
It's more fun to chase a pigeon than a real feathery stunner.

Gail Logan

GAIL

ATLANTIS ISLANDS LOST

On cloudy days when time seems far spent,
And life but a flickering flame,
The memory of time's past, of a civilization's remnants,
Glisten in the morning beams.

The shores where a million splendid reminders
Rest beneath the deep—a buried past,
A treasure far more magnificent than a pirate's bounty,
Lies hidden there.

To sail to far shores,
To envision a world where forgotten souls once
Worked and dreamed, is to see what lies before us.
Some say the present is a re-enactment of history.

The tree where wisdom's roots sank deep
Into the rudiments of civilization, was struck down here.
Islands once so gentle and peaceful in the morning light,
Evoke the memory of a fallen golden past.

Today they stand as silent memorials to
Their fiery beginning, when volcanic lava was
Thrown upon turbulent seas; where all seemed to cease
Until civilization's dying flame.
Marked the beginning of Paradise Regained.

Gail Logan

"A Hidden Place" and "Atlantis island Lost" express emotions and sympathies that one has after visiting places physically or sometimes only in spirit. When I was a child living in Wellfleet, I loved crossing Captain Tim's bridge where at low tide, I could look down and see the hundreds of little fiddler crabs scurrying about searching for food or waiting for the high tide to bring some delicious morsels their way. Today the fiddler crabs have all but disappeared from under that bridge, and so have the hundreds of terns that used to lay their eggs in the weeds and rushes on a bit of land overlooking the cove on Cove Rd. Those terns were so protective of their nests that they would menacingly dive down at any human intruder who dared approach their spring nesting grounds.

The horseshoe crabs still lay their eggs in the protective waters of Partridge's Beach just off Cove Rd., but Mrs Partridge, who used to live in the only house overlooking Partridge's Beach long since moved away. As for the house where she used to live so many years ago, before I was even born, the house is today threatened by rising waters due to climate change. Such is the Wellfleet I used to know. It's still beautiful but not quite the same. The Wellfleet Marina has changed the face of Wellfleet. Once a quiet little community for artists and those who wanted to live near the sea and commune with nature, the marina has enabled people from all over the East Coast or even farther away to converge upon this once quiet little getaway. Hotels, widened roads, and development have brought a new look to Wellfleet. Once there were just three or four houses on Cove Rd. including our family home, and the only houses on Indian Neck Rd were a few comfortable beach homes. There were no houses on Pilgrim Springs Rd. as I recall.

I have other memories of Wellfleet, especially of warm summer days when my friends and I joined up and headed for the back shore. Tucked beneath our arms were wooden surf boards our fathers had made us. We all were pretty good swimmers, and we respected the water perhaps more than most people who aren't used to living near the sea. We'd wait for low tide when we could swim out to a sand bar where incoming ocean waves crashed on the bar enabling us to catch them and ride them to shore. The activity was exhilarating and fun, and we would top the afternoon off by climbing a dune to see if there were any distant whales making their way in the sea parallel to shore. Before heading to home, we might take a swim in the clear fresh waters of Great Pond. On other days, we might just go to Long Pond where the town had anchored a big white raft just off shore from which people could swim to and dive. Another Wellfleet Pond I loved, was Gull Pond where gulls come to rest in the middle of its clear waters. Situated on Newcomb Hallow Beach Rd, you will see, if you row across it, that Gull Pond connects with two smaller woodland Ponds. It is said that Henry David Thoreau stayed for awhile in a house on the first pond connected to Gull Pond during his visit to Cape Cod culminating in his writing a book about his visit to the Cape. My family and friends liked to rent a boat and row across Gull Pond to swim and picnic at these three lovely ponds.

During late summer months, my school friends and I might pick wild blueberries or huckleberries growing along Cahoon's Hallow Rd, and my mother and I liked to gather wild beach plums together near Great Island at Duck Harbor so we could make jelly, usually enough for winter to share with friends. Those are the sunny carefree days that I remember—the summer square dances or record hops, the boat rides to Great island for a picnic barbecue, or the beginning of school when we had to say good by to friends we met during their summer visit to Cape Cod.

The end of the summer always seemed like a bit of a let down but no more so than when I realized that I had grown up and I was leaving Wellfleet too.

My family bought a second home in Rhode Island, and it was at the University of Rhode Island that I was exposed to ideas and a larger world than I'd ever known, even during that short time my brother, mother and I accompanied Dad when he was in the Air force. We first lived in Virginia near Langley Air Force Base and I had my first dog Skip, a cocker spaniel. We took him with us wherever we went, and I guess my obsession with animals and dogs started with him. He spent summers in Wellfleet with us, and he guarded our family home diligently when Mr. Dyer, who worked at the Wellfleet cemetery rode his bicycle by our house and Skip used to greet him with the loudest barking. Mr. Dyer, who was always smiling didn't seem to mind. He always was so jovial and kind. He had relatives in Wellfleet, and my family was sad when we learned he'd moved away.

My life has been full of changes of direction and environment but I struggle never to let any of it get me down. As a family we also lived in New York and Chicago for a short while and it was in Chicago when I attended High School there that I became interested in classical mythology. I also studied Latin at Lincoln School, Providence, RI and I was glad I did for it helped prepare me for study at the University of Rhode Island where I did my MA thesis on Mythology in Spenser's "Mutability Cantos". The influence of Ovid, that great Roman poet, found its way into some of my poems too, like "The Fallen","The Sun God Mourns", "Arachne", and "Echo and Narcissus." While my family was living in RI, we used to go to Wellfleet every weekend. But if the weather was really cold we'd stay home in Barrington, RI where we lived. I was stunned after returning from Canada where I have relatives and where I lived for two years to try to learn more French, to hear that my father took a job in GA. At that time my mother wasn't well. I know she missed her friends in RI and Cape Cod. I followed my parents to GA, and I took a job there so I could be near my mother but she died a short time later. That experience was a traumatic period in my life, and I must say I still struggle with the memory.

I stayed in GA and lived near my dad even after he remarried but I never returned to Wellfleet, only for one short visit to a friend who invited me to stay with her in Barnstable for a few days. We drove to Wellfleet and visited some of my old haunts. The visit almost seemed surreal, and I felt myself fighting back tears when I set foot on familiar turf. A lot had changed but then some things hadn't. We drove by our family's house and I saw the pink rambling roses in the yard that for years my mother had so carefully cared for. The tree house my dad had built for me, was still visible from the road, and it looked as if it was falling apart as did my brother's old sailboat left in the front yard to rot. My Dad didn't sell the Wellfleet property immediately after my mother died but since he was living in Georgia, he spent little time in Wellfleet, and decided finally to sell the property.

I knew I had to move on with life, so I began traveling to places I'd always wanted to see, like Mexico, the Caribbean and South America. The beaches and waters of Mexico and the Caribbean were beautiful but no more so than when I swam in Mexican waters at a white sand beach with the ancient Mayan ruins of Tulum in the background. I also visited Coba another ancient Mayan site, back in the jungle not far from Tulum. Also in the area, a day trip from Cancun, are the spectacular Pyramids and ruins of Chichen Itza. I've visited Chichen Itza several times and like the Mayan ruins of Tikal in Guatemala both are almost impossible to explore in one day, and one really needs a guide to do so. I've been told by experts that all of these ancient sites were used to worship the stars, sun, and planets. That sentiment certainly was there, when visiting Tikal, our guide advised our small group to be ready at 4:00 AM to follow him through the jungle so we could climb the Temple of the Sun and watch the sun rise. It was almost a mystical experience to see the sun slowly rise over jungle and listen to the world awake to the howls of howler monkeys and the joyous cries and calls of awakening birds of multiple species including toucans, Amazon parrots, and the majestic huge red Macaw. The Tikal Park rangers carefully guard these wild animals from poachers for so many of the birds and animals there are endangered species. As I watched the sun rise in this beautiful setting, I was convinced that this must be the way the world looked at the dawn of creation. In fact, the pyramid where we stood is also called "The Lost World".

Another place of great awe and wonder that I was fortunate enough to visit were the Andes Mountains in Peru. The city of Cusco (also Cuzco) there is fascinating for this once capital of the Inca Empire use to be a city laden in gold and there are legends telling of filigree gold gardens and temples covered in gold before the Spanish conquest ended it all. Yet the Spanish introduced some wonderful architecture to the area too and both cultures combine to make Cusco a unique experience. Some of the most ancient ruins in Cusco such as Quonkancha, the temple of the Sun and Moon and others are worth seeing but there are magnificent temples not far from this ancient city that are well worth seeing too. A visit to Machu Picchu, just a couple of hours train ride through the mountains, is well worth taking. I'll never forget my visit to that city, dubbed "Lost City of the Incas" perched high up in the Andes Mountains. I'll never forget climbing to the top of that city or gazing down over the edge of it. I held my breath and backed away a little as I gazed down at the steep drop thousands of feet below me. This city is not for the faint of heart, and one should really take a guide along if you want to climb the many terraces leading to the top of the city where you will get the most magnificent views of the mountains surrounding you and also of what is around you or thousands of feet below you.

When I felt brave enough to do it, I took time off from work and visited French Polynesia's Society Islands and other places. Since visiting England during college to attend a seminar on Spenser's poetry at Oxford University one summer, I managed to take a side trip into the English countryside and visit the fascinating ancient site of Stonehenge, an ancient calendar. After reading a book by a prominent mathematician, who has the numbers to prove it, I learned that almost all great ancient monuments, including those of ancient Mexico, S. America, Egypt Greece, and Rome, embody a record of the heavens and astronomy for thousands of years, long before the advent of Christianity. Most if not all were used as calendars. I was so enticed by things ancient all over the world that I decided to visit the Society Islands in the S. Pacific where I heard there were remains of ancient marae or stone structures and platforms on Huahine. The Bishop Museum in Honolulu had just excavated them and visiting the remains on Huahine was the next thing to paradise. At that time, Huahine had just one hotel, very lovely, charming but modern in a rustic sort of way with thatched roof bungalows and an open air thatch roof screened in dining room and a spring fed swimming pool. It was well run, clean and situated just back from the lagoon. I loved listening to the Polynesian people singing and playing instruments in the hotel at night, and I was charmed by the singing coming from a nearby church Sunday morning as I breathed in the sea air and smelled the jasmine and tiare blossoms while riding a bike on a dirt island road. Much as I loved visiting Huahine, fascinating too was Tahiti, a less remote version of Huahine. I associated Tahiti with Captain James Cook, and I was moved to visit the site where he first landed. Interesting too were the tales surrounding the famous Mutiny on the Bounty. Some of the islanders are descended from mutineers who married island women only to be hunted down and taken back to England to be tried and hanged for mutiny. How sad, I thought to have to leave this paradise so tragically.

My visits to the S. Pacific didn't end then for I also visited the North Island of New Zealand where I toured the Bay of Islands, Ninety Mile Beach, and one of the most beautiful places I've ever seen: Cape Reinga is a high cliff overlooking the place where the Tasman Sea meets the Pacific Ocean. The New Zealand Maori people believe Cape Reinga is where the spirits of the dead depart for their journey to the land from whence they came. In other parts of Polynesia, like Easter Island, that land hidden in legend and mystery, is referred to as Hiva but I suppose other parts of Polynesia may give it a different name.

The feelings I had when visiting Cape Reinga are not unlike the feelings I sometimes had as a child in Wellfleet when I stood on a high dune and gazed out to sea where the sea and sky seemed to meet with no line separating one from the other. Such a scene inspires the imagination for people I knew told me that directly across the sea from where I stood is Spain and Portugal. After reading books on the legendary island of Atlantis, I was convinced that the remains of Atlantis lie buried somewhere off the Straits of Gibraltar and the Canary Islands not far from Spain. Strange remains have been found in that area but nothing definite yet is confirmed to be remnants of the legendary island of Atlantis that reputedly sank over 12,000 years ago.

The Atlantic and Pacific Oceans often are places of baffling mystery. The mutineers aboard the Bounty who didn't stay in Tahiti joined Fletcher Christian aboard the Bounty and lowered Captain Bligh and his followers into an open boat to fend for themselves before making their way to

Pitcairn Island. Bligh and his followers miraculously made it to Australia thousands of miles away. As for Fletcher Christian and his group, when in 1789, they arrived at Pitcairn Island, they discovered that their refuge was off by several hundred miles from the place it was supposed to be as shown on nautical maps making them safe from discovery by the British Admiralty. The mission of the Bounty to transport breadfruit plants from Tahiti to the Caribbean may have failed but other British ships came to Tahiti and transported the breadfruit plants to their Caribbean destination. Several hundred years later, when I visited an old plantation in the mountains overlooking the Caribbean Sea in Jamaica, I was served breadfruit at lunch, and was told how it ended up on the menu.

When I returned to Auckland from the Bay of Islands where in a day or so I was to fly to Sydney, I was fascinated by that city in many ways. For me Auckland seemed to have not just the atmosphere of a sophisticated modern city but rural charm as well. Cows in a city park grazed nonchalantly on a hill overlooking Auckland Harbor, and I understand that they were well cared for by municipality representatives who probably thought a cow or two might bring a peaceful aura to a busy city. Since I live in rural GA where an occasional cow wanders into my yard, I was pleased with the Auckland arrangement. Visiting the Auckland Museum, also was a treat. I enjoyed the exhibition of Maori dancing—they were great, and I was nearly blown over to see a stuffed flightless bird, the Moa, now extinct almost bigger than I am. I love birds, and to think that this magnificent bird is now extinct was not only sad but depressing. Also sad is the knowledge that the beautiful Kauri trees that I admired and that once were so abundant in New Zealand forests, are growing scarce these days.

From Auckland it was on to Sydney, Australia where my first glimpse of everything was dominated by the beautiful Harbor and the fascinating architecture of the Sydney Opera House. I took a city tour, where we made a stop at the beautiful botanical gardens and Bondi Beach where people were enjoying the water. Like any other large city, Sydney has its shops, office buildings and hotels but it was near the harbor water front that its history unraveled itself. Sydney first was established as a penal colony and the stone fortresses, and cubicles along the water front now are turned into smart looking stores and coffee shops. I especially enjoyed Sydney's art galleries and museums for many of them focus on the culture of modern day Sydney as well as that of Aboriginal people who believe in the dreamtime, and consider all living creatures comprising the world to be equal—a beautiful philosophy today since so many species throughout the world are becoming extinct because of man's development and expansion into their habitat. The dreamtime, if I interpret it correctly, also includes a concept that the past, present and future are one.

Not far from Sydney are the Blue Mountains and Jamison Valley where I saw some lovely exotic large and colorful birds as well as some fascinating natural mountainous structures including one dubbed "The three sisters". My time in Australia was short though. I was sorry that I couldn't make it up to Queensland's Gold Coast where my mother's brother lived. After my mom died we corresponded for a long time. My uncle came to visit my mother in RI a few years before she died—that was the last time I ever saw him since he now is deceased too.

From Sydney, it was on to Fiji. After landing in Nadi, I took a boat out to a nearly uninhabited island off Nadi. There were about 20 people in our group and we enjoyed a stay there. Everyone occupied the time there differently. Some walked around and explored this lovely desert island atoll. I swam and snorkeled to my heart's content for the beach was beautiful and along with just a few others, we had the lagoon to ourselves. In the distance, across the lagoon, was another island. I'm not sure what is was called but it looked remote, beautiful and mountainous. When it was time to leave the island, I climbed aboard the small boat with my belongings beside me and sat at the boat's edge so I could dangle my feet over the boat's side.

We definitely were at sea, and Nadi was nowhere in sight. I was sun burned for having been in the sun so long. I'd enjoyed my time on that little island but I looked forward to some comfortable accommodations at the hotel in Nadi. The sun was beginning to sink in the sky and the boat seemed to pitch a little as the wind picked up and spray washed over the prow of the boat. I held my breath and thought, if the wind picks up much more we're out of luck. Finally the lights of Nadi appeared in the darkening sky, and I knew we'd made it to more peaceful waters within a lagoon. When we reached land, a hotel rep picked me and my belongings up and I made it back to my hotel—rather late where I showered, ordered a big steak sandwich with sides and looked forward to another adventure.

It takes courage to live and perhaps even more courage to love and always to be kind to others wherever you go or visit. When I write my poems, whether they be about people, my travels or animals, I try to keep that thought in mind. The succeeding poems whether they are about subjects I've already written about or subjects yet to come, all illustrate that philosophy.

Gail Logan

BOVINE FRIENDS

Matilda and Jasmine are dear indeed
For they like being seen by those who welcome
Them it seems.
Although unaware of their ample girth,
The girls don't care if people stare.
Jasmine and Matilda know they are rare as rubies,
So why shouldn't one compare one lovely cow to the other beauty?
People are fascinated by the girls'
Dainty mystique, and bovine feats.
Matilda is white and spotted black while her friend,
Jasmine is chocolate brown and sweet for a fact.
Although their hooves are large, the girls drift through
Time as if they were in a fairy world sublime.
They flit from one pasture to the next,
And sometimes they emerge from nowhere,
Which is a bit of a scare if one isn't prepared
To observe fairy-like bovines walk on air.
They use their tinkling cow bells to let you know where they are going.
If it's raining or snowing, they'll head for the barn.
After all, they do live on a farm.
But they'd rather be pasture haunting on any warm sunny day,
And that's where you'll usually find them munching grass or eating hay.

Gail Logan

THE DOOR CLOSED UPON YOU

Torn from your earth home by bulldozers,
Suffocated, lifeless, I find you mole.
Your blind eyes sunken, your small form limp,
Asleep near my back yard

I pick you up and caress your cold body
In my warm hands.
I gently stroke your fur as if in vain to awaken you.
I touch your paws that look like tiny fingers,
And I feel a bond between us.

I grasp the enormity of your small life,
And your cruel exit from a hostile world
Where habitat daily is encroached upon;
Closing the door upon you and your wilderness world.

Gail Logan

GAIL

THE WASTELAND FORGOTTEN

Speak gently of me in this silent world of madness.
Let no harsh words be expressed in thought or deed.
Let remembrance be sweet like the silent dreams we dream
Each day to escape this world of grief.
Bring me yonder to a distant place
Where I again may see the grayness of that stark sea
Set amidst childhood's silent gray horizon.
Speak gently of me now as I
Enter that realm of everlasting grace.
Bring me nearer to Him who waits beyond this place.
Hasten me onward towards perfection's peace
Let me leave the wretchedness of this world's endless defeat.

Gail Logan

LAST WORDS IN THE DIARY
OF A WHITE WITCH

Last night she saw him standing there as he had before but
He was gone when she awoke from the dream.
Only his touch and embrace remain in thought.
Some say his ship was wrecked at sea but today it is anchored in the cove.
Tonight she will surely rendezvous with him again.
She longs to journey to the endless deep.
She longs to cross over to the other side
Where all is enveloped in eternal stillness.
Time has set her free.
But the abyss hidden in morning sunlight is widening.
Only his love will break the spell of enmity's shadow.
The gray outline of dawn has given way to eternal sunrise.
The life she once knew is gone. She is ready to join him.
She recalls the words to a song she sang long ago.
Its melody like the sight of the rising morning tide envelops her.
"Let me be with the one who loves me now—
The one whose ship lies
Anchored in the cove below the crimson horizon."

Gail Logan

THE LOVE WITHIN

It's all within her the love she feels for him.
Each thought so kind so gentle yet sublime is never lost
Within the mystery of time, not easy to define yet simple
And without sin she loves him gently as each hour begins.
Even when she walks a path alone,
She knows he's with her as if he is coming home.
His arms are still around her as if he at last has found her.
No curse of hate can separate those who love from afar.
No fortress walls or enemy's call can force her to desert.
For within Love's circle is a track, a secret pact that defies lies and
Society's ties holding a world in disarray.
They walk together silently each reaching within the other,
One Soul to make them better, a light to make them one together.
For that silent Love is held together by a higher peace, a selfless lease
When two beings are released in freedom, they always shall be together.
True love never can separate or bring decay even when shadows of
Death might bring dismay.

Gail Logan

BROTHER WOLF

Brother wolf raises his pointed nose towards the bloody sky.
With a howling bellow,
He lets our an anguished cry.
He knows that in the distance
His fellows far away,
Are hunted to near extinction,
And are but helpless prey.
Desperate to escape,
The wolves race from the Alaskan rim.
No noise is more terrifying
Than pursuing aircrafts'cruel din.
Silently each canine falls
From a shot fired from above.
And brother wolf howls instinctively
In final farewell
To those he loves

Gail Logan

THE SHADOW

She may be found walking alone along the shores of a land unseen.
Her story is familiar to those who have heard the unseen ocean's
Roar or been touched by the sea's mysterious beauty.

She whispers of the past: of lovers' tales or ships which once sailed
Upon the deep. I've seen her only once.

She smiles with contentment. She agilely steps
Back from waves that seethe upon the jagged rocks of eternity.
The icy fingers of foamy spray caress the rocks, beckoning her to
Become at one with the brilliant blue sea.

She stops momentarily. She gazes at the distant horizon. She
Watches the sea's restless beauty wallow in loneliness like a light
Searching in the darkness.

She turns. She continues walking along the shores of the endless
Beach until distance enfolds the image of her.

Gail Logan

GAIL

42

TOAD'S RAINY DAY

He dodges raindrops one at a time,
Soggy missles that combine to create
A puddle of mud and slime, where
Toad stays until he finds a
A path and garden pool where
He rejuvenates and takes a bath
He then sips drink from a well formed
Bud enclosing nectar so sublime that
Toad is quite sure he's been transported in time.
He wobbles a bit then snaps at a flea,
As gleeful elves and fairies watch and laugh
From the leaves of a tree.
The rain then stops, and a groggy toad,
Makes his way homeward bound
Before burrowing into the ground so deep,
Where he sleeps and sleeps.
Toad then awakes, hops from his hole,
Has tea with a bee, and waits patiently
For another rainy reprieve.

Gail Logan

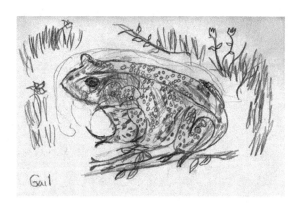

COYOTE'S LOST WORLD

Huehuecoyoti searches for a land of long ago.
He hears it in leaves rustling in the breeze
Or in his ancestor's ghostly call that
He mimics at sunset or sunrise especially during clear days of fall.
Once worshipped as a god by the Aztec and Inca people,
Coyote, Lord of the Sun, longs for
The sublime time when they ruled his world.
The remains of their great temples and palaces are awesome
Reminders of that lost clime.
Today Coyote's often gaunt thin image wanders too close
To those who have lost the ways of former days.
He cries for the Gate of the House of the Sun again to open
To honor the mystery of the planets and stars,
And to rejuvenate a natural world now so lost and quite marred.

Gail Logan

COYOTE, LORD OF THE
HOUSE OF THE SUN

Huehuecoyoti's mythical dance of mirth and joy,
Proves him to be no coward or decoy.
At sunrise his image becomes at one
With the sun's glow, and his musical howl
touches the sky's fiery domain before he again enters
A strange modern world where he sees
A dog straining behind a fence in the attempt
To answer the call and join coyote in preventing Nature's fall.
The natural world coyote looks for is shrinking
But this harbinger of an earlier time,
Bravely stands at sunset and faithfully calls for a better clime*.

Gail Logan

BIG FOX (HE WAS PART COYOTE)

Fox says hello in many ways.
His whine or bark says if he is scared or brave.
He wags his tail as if to say,
"I'm glad to be here today.
I'm happy to be loved and free
So that I may walk alongside you
Within the forest and trees."
No day goes by without him showing
How much he loves
The simple things that keep him going:
A home and warm bed, good food and friends,
And a lap to place his gentle head
Upon so his pointed velvety ears
May be scratched at the end of day.
Fox is more than a dog to me.
He is a true friend who never lets me forget
How much life there is to live, and how wonderful it is
Just to be.

Fox continued

Angel dog is here today. I feel his protective love in many ways.
His bright red coat catches light of day as fearlessly he bounds
Within a rainbow haze.
His soft brown eyes reflect that light as silently
He continues life's fight.
I know his life never met its end. His bark is heard again and again.
A whisper on the wind or a raindrop falling,
indicate to me that fox is calling.
Sometimes I try to follow his trail but then I realize I'd only fail.
His paw prints are invisible you see.

There is a gap between us as great as a sea.
Someday where friends are united within that veil,
With a hug or a wag of a tail.
I'll feel his gentle head beneath my hand as together
We listen to life's plan.
Fox is here today.
Although I can't see him,
I know he never went away

Gail Logan

ALONE IN THE FOREST DEEP (RED WOLF)

Golden Red lives life courageously but with regret.
He wishes only to be lost in the Forests depths.
When his mother left him for eternal sleep,
Instinct told Golden Red that he should not succumb to defeat.
The survival instincts of coyote, wolf and fox were his, and
The primeval mystery of their world surrounded him.
The wilderness spirit he embodied was his refuge.
The memory of his noble ancestors,
Gave Golden Red the courage to live for
He emerged from the shelter of trees and climbed a great hill and waited.
Then skyward he pointed his nose up and howled until
The moonlight spilled around him,
And revealed ghostly tracks where
The distant sublime, sometimes bloody legacy of the pack,
Was etched in memory of one final attack.

Gail Logan

LOVE IS A FOOL

Love deals a sorry hand
When the trail twists and turns
And only tears prevail.
Look up. He's reflected there in the
World around you as if his arms like
Branches still encompassed you.
You hear his voice in the music of
The forest wind.
Then you turn around and see only the
The forest dim.
If you could but follow him
Wherever he went,
You could take his hand in yours and tell
Him not to lament.
Love has its twists and turns
So perhaps its time to reverse direction and show
Him your intent.
Love is a fool for one so lost and alone as you.
"Dream on?" you tell yourself.
"Is it better to be alone than to die?"
And so you drift through the specter of trees
And sky, haunted by sweet words and lies
That tease and hide.
Love died for you the day he went away.
"Don't be a fool" a whispering pine
Conveys, "you'll love again,
And look for him no more
Amidst the misery of a lover's dismay.
You'll laugh instead and say:
He need never return to me again.
The man I once loved is gone. Old memories
Must end!"

Gail Logan

THE FLORIDA PANTHER

So elusive you seem to those looking for you.
Only your cries late at night connect us
With your world so out of sight.
Today your journey has taken you far from the one you once knew.
Gone is your world of endless forests deep and narrow streams to cross.
Today your paw prints seem invisible and quite lost.
You have entered a distant hollow so remote it seems
That one can't convey such an image even in dreams.
Your tawny form must connect with landscape so astounding
That you confound those who stumble across your path,
Only to discover that you blend too well with the grass.
You have disappeared entirely from the many seeking you.
Distant, even feared,
You move farther away each day from encroaching civilization
That simply won't go away

Gail Logan

NOCTURNAL SURVIVOR

With silvery gray coat and pink pointed snout, the little
Gray opossum is busy and about.
He glides beneath the still pale moonlight,
And hears a conflicting call of the wild tonight.
He stops to consider an option or two.
Should he dare cross the highway in search of leftover food?
The remains of burgers and fries
Or a succulent pizza might relieve the tedium of his daily supply
Of wild roots and climbing ivy shoots.
Opossum reassesses his travel plans.
He turns from the busy highway that might become his last stand.
He heads back through the trees and tells himself that daily survival really
is a breeze.
He nibbles on a mushroom or two, then casually steps around a friendly
snake in view.
He glides over barely concealed things:
A broken bottle thrown in the grass, and then finds crumbs hidden in
the trash.
With tail held high, opossum continues on his way.
He makes a quick detour through a backyard or two
Until he finds his hollow in a tree where he goes to bed for a snooze.
Later as the sun rises in the sky, opossum is grateful to be alive
Yesterday didn't mean the end of life's path only the beginning of
A better road leading to today's greener grass.

Gail Logan

DRAGON IN THE SKY

He is a cloud above me, a dragon in the sky.
When I turn to look behind me, I see his image down there beside me:
A snake so miniscule, he hardly seems real at all.
Who are you? I wonder as I compare this little form
To the diaphanous one above me.
His ancestor's image with flaggy wings and mighty tail
Evokes the memory of one who terrorized those
Who dared prevail against his ancient vale.
Yet he is mere mist. It is hard to believe that he once
Ruled this swampy land on which I stand.
He raises his horny head, and looks fiercely down upon me as
Quickly he floats beyond me.
Such a contrast is he to the little snake who
Uncertainly gazes up at me.
I cautiously step around him so as not to step upon him.
His intricately patterned skin
Blends so well with colorful leaves of fall, he hardly seems real at all.
"Good day my friend", I say respectfully as I pass beyond him.
The little snake quickly slithers away surprised to have
Made my acquaintance and to have been part of my day.

Gail Logan

FELINE PATH

Mama Kitty, Baby Scat and Sam, are a lost but rambunctious feline band.
During the day, they roll and play with careless display.
At night they follow along a river path where
Crickets play and moonbeams light the way.
Across the hollow, through long marsh grass, they come to a secret place
Where dragons weep, and green lizards withdraw into tunnels deep.
Mice scurry and hide as the band moves forward.
They dig down into new mown hay where felines pause with curious paws,
Until an old gray opossum reminds the band of approaching dogs.
Swiftly the lost kitties make their way to a silvery glade where they roll and
Yowl and scream like sinners until they smell a familiar scent.
There's no need to repent or dream of rich cream and tuna supreme.
They've found the right path homeward where
Dinner awaits the felines you see, and where each kitty is loved
And has plenty to eat.

Gail Logan

THE SAND DUNE

Adrift beneath and high above the sea,
Is a world before one, a view of infinity.
Below, the empty beach stretches far into the distance.
But the sea alone takes hold of the imagination and sets one free.
It's hard to move away from this gray stark scene.
Like the lighthouse far behind, one is pulled into the scene,
As if one is part of the dream:
The sea's change of mood and seasonal clime is an environment
Where ships come and go amidst this ancient flow,
And where the whale's distant call echoes
Primeval music prior to the Fall.
Yes, there was a time when Nature ruled
Land and sea and man was content to live amidst it all with harmony and
dignity.
Now all has changed.
What is left of untamed Nature's world
Is in turmoil as man encroaches on sacred ground
Polluting air and waters all around.
The whale's high pitched cry has meaning today.
He laments what man has brought to the Earth:
Terrible wars and wanton decay,
A disregard for everything in his way.
Like the whale, I too cry for an earlier time,
A world of sublime natural beauty, a world devoid of evil and decline.

Gail Logan

It was on the way to Hawaii from Fiji that I began to realize why I had undertaken the adventure I'd embarked upon. I felt the islands of the Pacific and the Atlantic Oceans held the key to uncovering the truth about the legendary Atlantis that reputedly disappeared in the Atlantic Ocean about 12,000 years ago, and another great island continent, Mu, often confused with Atlantis, that disappeared in the Pacific Ocean about the same time. According to scholars, Mu often is referred to as "The lands of the West," but it is in the Codex Cortesianus, an old Maya book, written 5,000 years ago that a more precise record of Mu is given as, "a land of earth hills and rolling plains" that existed for over 50,000 years ago but vanished during a cataclysm 12,000 years ago. Another record, one of the oldest papyrus rolls in existence was written in the reign of Pharaoh Sent of the second Egyptian dynasty 4571 BC. The papyrus roll tells of how the Pharaoh sent an expedition to the west in search of traces of the western land from which the ancient Egyptian settlers arrived thousands of years earlier from "the motherland" carrying with them the knowledge of this highly advanced western civilization Mu. After five years of searching for this legendary land of the west, the expedition returned empty handed. Yet today, allusions to Mu's ancient existence are found all over the world. In the old Buddhist Temple of Lhasa, there is an inscription written about 2,000 BC recalling the destruction of Mu, "when the star of Bal fell on the place where there is now only sea and sky". In another ancient manuscript, The Troano Manuscript written in the Yucatan between 1,500 to 3,000 years ago, it states that the "lands of the west" or the "motherland", lay to the west of America, and the Troano Manuscript gives a precise description of Mu's devastation 12,000 years ago.

While Mu is referred to as "the motherland" or "the lands of the west", the most ancient name for Atlantis was "the Saturnian continent", a place "beyond the Pillars of Hercules" or the Strait of Gibraltar. As this land reputedly extended far into the Atlantic Ocean, it is understandable that some scholars believe that the two continents, Mu and Atlantis, thousands of years ago, were connected by a S American inland sea connecting the lands of the Atlantic and Pacific Oceans. In fact, there are ancient maps in existence today showing this. Today that inland sea is nothing more than a great river known as the Amazon River. The ancient inhabitants of Mu and Atlantis reputedly worshipped the Sun, and since Mu, the older of the two civilizations, colonized Atlantis, it is understandable that the people of Atlantis as well as those of Mexico, Central and S.America—and even early inhabitants of N America as well as the people of ancient Egypt worshipped the sun as well. But there are other similarities. The pyramids of Ancient Mexico and S America are similar to those of Egypt in many ways: the people of ancient S, America and Egypt both mummified their dead, a practice probably originating in "the motherland."

Since I am a great devotee of the writings of James Churchward, and since I use his non- fiction books often as background in writing my works of fiction, I take what he has to say about Mu quite seriously. What he writes about makes perfect sense if you think about it. He claims that the islands of the vast Pacific Ocean are remnants of what is left of the great continent of Mu. Take for instance, Easter Island, that small mysterious island in the Pacific just off the coast of Chile. Why would ancient residents of such a small island carve such curious figures weighing tons unless they were doing so to honor something which to this day remains unfinished? According to the late archaeologist, W J Thompson, there is a tablet found on Easter Island that when deciphered, reads as follows: A legend tells the following, "This island had once been a part of a great continent crossed with many roads beautifully paved with flat stones." That continent could only be Mu and work on the carvings of Easter Island's curious figures weighing tons, and one 70 feet in length, suddenly broke off when this large continent of which Easter Island and other islands of the Pacific are remnants, broke apart due to a cataclysm. On the coast of Chile curious figures similar to those of Easter Island are found too. Where did they come from? Obviously, parts of Chile and Easter Island both had a connection with a continent in the Pacific known as Mu. More recent discoveries substantiate this claim. After leaving Fiji on an evening flight bound for the Hawaiian Islands, it was early morning, when in the distance I gazed down and saw the Hawaiian islands strung out as if they all were neatly placed on a map. As I gazed downward, I wondered what lay beneath the sea near these islands, and why after flying over thousands of miles of uninhabited ocean, they suddenly appeared out of nowhere.

Again, I thought of the legendary continent of Mu that was reputed to be 5000 miles long and 3000 miles wide. Was this and other Pacific Islands, all that remained of a once great continent's legendary power and beauty? Some oceanographers and geologists say that halfway between North America and the Hawaiian Islands are three pyramids under 2,600 feet of water that are of the same shape and form as the great pyramids of Giza. In fact, they even have taken underwater photographs of them. Then there is the curious discovery made in 1972 corroborated by UN diplomat Farida Iskoviet and US Army Sgt William Fennel that confirms there is an ancient sunken city lying between the islands of Maui and Oahu.

The cataclysm that destroyed not just Mu but Atlantis as well may be attributed mainly to geologic instability and flooding. Yet there is the possibility too that an asteroid falling from the sky may also have contributed to the devastation of both. The line of devastation from the sunken Atlantis is reflected by sunken ruins found along the east coast of Florida to, Hispaniola, Puerto Rico, the Antilles, Trinidad and to an ancient sunken city discovered off the Cuban coast. Yet the destruction brought about by Atlantis' sinking is seen in buried remnants of ancient human construction along the Grand Bank of Bermuda. as well as off the coast of Andros, the largest island in the Bahamas and in the extreme northwest portion of Bimini revealing a vast sunken expanse of pavement, all hand cut and without a doubt manmade.

I live in Georgia and this state and neighboring states surrounding it have a link with a very ancient past of 17,000 years of continuous human habitation. Many different Indian cultures lived here for thousands of years. But it is during the Mississippian period that the great mound builders left their mark here and in other states within the area. The Ocmulgee National Monument in Macon is an excellent example of that culture. In fact, the Ocmulgee National Monument had the largest archaeological dig in American history when in the 1930's, with over

800 men working and discovering three million artifacts— including two sun discs seen on display in the Ocmulgee Monument museum. Did the ancients in Macon, GA and surrounding area worship the sun?

In Eatonton, GA is another example of ancient culture. At ground level, Rock Eagle looks just like another pile of rocks. Obviously, this monument like so many others in Peru and elsewhere, like the 1,348 foot long, 3 foot high effigy mound in Adams County Ohio, (Great Serpent Mound) it is meant to be viewed from the air. Rock Eagle measures 102 feet from head to tail, and it is composed of probably several hundred thousand quartz rocks. Rock Eagle, it's said was constructed 6000 years ago, before the Creeks settled the area 2000 years later. See Bill Boyd "Ancient Effigy is Worthy Cause", The Macon Telegraph, Feb 11, 1990.

There is another bird rock effigy of a hawk 12 miles away from it, probably constructed about the same time—although I feel the two bird effigies are probably older than that. Since the ancients believed in the gods, obviously they were trying to gain their attention. For after the destruction of Mu and Atlantis, for thousands of years, the world must have been a bleak place. According to the late James Churchward, the bird symbol honored in Mu and Atlantis mythology and religion was always a symbol of the Creator. Were those who built the bird effigies appealing to the Creator for help?

There may be some who prefer to shut one's mind to what happened in the distant past but I am among those who prefer to keep mine open, for in doing so we may be able to help prevent the next cataclysm.

Gail Logan

SQUIRREL WHIRL

They gracefully bound from
The limbs of a tree or circle 360 degrees before they measure
A fall as if length didn't matter at all.
Such is the family of gray squirrels who live and rest
With such quiet success that their chattering and squealing
Only express how well they are feeling.
How grateful they are for the bounty of a yard:
The acorns that fall from oak leaves or the
Pine nuts they pluck from giant pine trees that are eaten
With relish but sometimes embellish a humble nest of rest.
They live each day as if it were their last.
Yet they never succumb to defeat if a family member goes missing.
Instead they sing a high pitched
Lament so encompassing that the heavens above
Must hear mournful trumpeting.
Each chattering quest begins with courage not fret
Within this changing world
Where all things great and small, must never be taken
For granted at all.

Gail Logan

THE SHAGGY BAND
OF WONDERLAND

"Every dog must have his day" but that's not why
The sheepdog ran away.
After Bo Beep carelessly lost her sheep,
While crossing a busy street,
Shaggy the sheepdog knew that
Every dog must earn his keep, so he returned, and
With his superior nose for sniffing out territory,
He led the clan of bleating beasts
Away from well meaning sheep shearers and frightening meat thieves
To where sheep never would be served up as entrees or delectable treats.
Without a single mournful bah or bleat of adieu,
Shaggy and the woolly flock, passed an aghast Bo Beep who watched
As the dog led the woolly band through
Alice's looking glass into wonderland.

Gail Logan

ALLIGATORS BANNED

The alligator is in the way these days.
He hasn't gotten the message that's being conveyed,
through the media and press.
That negative news about him
Won't give him a rest.
Where does a big gator go for food, recreation and play?
The roads near the swamp are too wide, and Gator
Often collides with cars with people inside who'd just as soon see him die.
Okay, he's often seen as a lot of trouble, and mean but that doesn't mean
He deserves to be chopped up for alligator fritters or his hide used for a
fancy look in pocketbooks or alligator slippers. Those things just give him
the jitters.
He once had Disneyworld to himself but that was before the place was
built, and Gator had nowhere else to go to find a space that offered swampy
silt or a lake.
Then the tourists came knocking on the door, and Gator got in trouble
For mistaking people for an alligator shuttle offering him a one way trip to
Gator Fantasy land that ended in a trip to No Where Land
Where alligators are dead, and relegated to deep sand pits after carrying
Off a person, or biting off someone's hand.
"Oh for the good ole days", mourns Gator as he sits in the corner of an
undiscovered swamp and dreams away the hours, before he glides through
the murky waters, afraid of those who might discover him, and view him
as something they don't want.
He tries to forget the many times he's been hunted down for no good
reason at all, like
reason at all, like the bungled attempt to grab a human intruder's leg that
sent Gator away, relegated to a farm for a permanent stay.
Maybe Gator has seen his day but if man reaches too far into primitive
land, gator may not be the one who vanishes in the end.
For the call of the wild is still there, and men must learn to be more

generous and answer the call by leaving a little space for others, especially gators— after all.

This world is getting overcrowded each day, and soon man may be the only one in the way.

Gail Logan

Gail

FREE FLYING BUMBLE BEES

Buzzwal, Bitsy and Bubba are a trio of free flying traveling bumble bees.
They know what they want in a day's work, and travel the low lying hedges
and rows
Of sweet peas without thinking of any sort of planned strategy.
It all comes naturally you see,
for these bees are a force of nature without Bee degrees in high flying
honeybee robbery.
On the contrary, they're on an honest stealing spree.
They case out each garden and don't expect a pardon from observing
insects that scour the nearby skies in search of unguarded gardens and
honey bee hives.
Buzzwal shoots from one black stripe of his fuzzy insect bumble bee hide
in time to scare off insects that linger too close to Bitsy or Bubba as the
three steal honey from nearby hives.
Such daring excitement only adds zest and vigor to a day's work well done, and
Bitsy and Bubba retreat just in time into the leaves of a peach tree, and
Wait for Buzzwal to complete his daring escapade and join up with them
making three.
They then check out what's been done during the course of a day until
A nosy bear wanders upon the scene, and attempts to cash in on the day's
sweet spree.
Just as an offending paw reaches for the bounty inside the nest,
The three ornery bumble bees sting his nose instead, and
The crying intruder quickly dashes away from the bumble bees' stash of
the day.

Gail Logan

MARY ANN THE FRIENDLY SHARK

Mary Ann isn't the kind of shark that looks for something to
Tear apart.
She's strong, beautiful and agile to behold and if a shark can be
Called refined, Mary Ann is definitely that kind.
She's quick witted and smart and knows her own survival depends
On distinguishing between who's who and who's what,
Especially if it's someone on a surf board or a seal too close to shore.
She really doesn't want to hurt anyone, and she doesn't want to even a
score.
She never used to hunt seals, they're not her favorite meal but
Since they left the Arctic for warmer waters, seals are taking her meals.
Cape Cod bluefish that can live almost anywhere in Atlantic waters are a
Favorite of Mary Ann's so fishermen beware don't let Mary Ann get in the
Way by getting snagged in a net in the bay. She knows what she is doing,
She's only after lunch so give her a little slack. Mary Ann won't attack,
and she
definitely won't be back.
But since she is susceptible to hunger these days and she smells the day's
catch
From miles away, she'll follow that boat to the dock or shore, hoping for
a handout
In the form of leftovers thrown overboard.
Mary Ann is a lady. She really doesn't want to offend.
She knows her survival depends on being a good girl.
So please cooperate and follow proper etiquette.
Don't swim at night. She's apt to find that time of day,

A reason for picking a fight for anything that moves towards her in the night.

Above all, try to love her.

Forget about eating shark fin soup—it may seem like a delicacy to a few but to Mary Ann it invites revenge, and that simply breaks all the rules.

Gail Logan

Gail

THE BAT IN THE CAVE

He hides from the world most of the time but that doesn't means he's idle.
He sleeps in a cave during the day for he usually is exhausted after a night's
Work of eating thousands of mosquitoes and insects in sight.
If you think he's not lovely to behold you are quite mistaken.
Without his huge black satiny wings sometimes hiding his face,
He really is the image of a puppy lost in space. His soft black fur coat,
And his huge dark lost looking eyes break one's heart inside.
If you'd like to take him home you can't for this little puppy is quite bold
and his
Bat wings move so fast that you'd never be quick enough to get a hold of
This elusive, delicate
Soulful fellow whose little pink tongue and soft velvety pointed ears,
Make one realize there is nothing to fear.
His lot in life often is a sad one though. Men have intruded too deeply
into his
Lost cave world. Civilization has brought disease and misery to his life.
He's not even welcome in attics or the belfry and the likes.
Often a creature derided in books and horror films, he should instead be
Respected, for if he could talk, this little creature, no doubt could tell us a lot.
With the pale hue of moonlight painting his wings, he is a creature of
gentleness and hope,
A symbol of what lies beyond but might never be found.

Gail Logan

66

MOTH OUTSIDE THE DOOR

Some say moths and butterflies are messengers from beyond.
The only moth near my outside light last night was a tiny white paper thin
Little image less than a quarter inch across that at a distance might be
mistaken
For a large snowflake left over from winter frost.
Her tiny form asleep, resting on a green
Gardenia leaf blended perfectly with a nearby blooming blossom.
Was she being a messenger today? And if so what was she trying to convey?
Her world is shrinking, and the climate she long has known somehow has
flown.
She looked quite alone and vulnerable on that little leaf:
So delicate was she, she could have been in a dream,
She seemed at peace but out of place as if the world she
Wanted to fly to wasn't there anymore but somehow had been erased.
I hesitated before I turned away helpless to aid her
Amidst all the corruption and confusion that has crept into this world
today.
I wanted to ask her to stay but perhaps that was asking her to do too much.
I knew I had to pray for the world she knows has lost its way.

Gail Logan

SEAL

Whiskers the seal likes to snooze in deep sea water.
But lately that activity seems to be much harder.
Ever since seals moved from the Arctic to Cape Cod,
Whiskers and his friends have to be on guard.
Shark predators defend what little they have so seals
Seem out of place on the Cape and other nearby Atlantic escapes.
The fish aren't always abundant and there are too many hungry
Mouths around for seals to feel secure and at peace.
Too many horrific accidents occur when seals and sharks clash and
Fight over food and territory.
Lately too many of Whiskers good friends have found themselves
On the losing end.
The sharks and seals both know that man is the real culprit here.
The currents and weather patterns have changed,
And man's intrusion and overfishing into sacred fishing territory
For seals and sharks alike have caused the dreadful plight.
Even when Whiskers and a few of his seal friends politely but
Grudgingly accept from fisherman, a transfer home to the Arctic's door,
Tears fill Whisker's eyes for he knows life there won't be home anymore.

Gail Logan

THE PIRATE AND THE ENCHANTRESS

Her bewitching blue eyes deep as the sea he loved, met his mesmerized gaze beneath a thousand white apple blossoms covering them like a haze. Hesitantly he reached for her slender hand that would bind her to him as The wind blew her long golden hair like a sail caught in a willful breeze. She knew that loving him would bring death.

Yet she accepted the bond resulting in unfulfilled lives.

His was a cruel destiny for powerful men determined to destroy This young man who found his fortune against their command, By taking from them when he saw a need, and giving to others without greed, stood in his way.

Evil pursued them like an angry squall ready to take their lives as it did Their child.

"Let me come with you today" she said as he left her to go back to sea. For days after, she stood on a high dune awaiting his return from sea. When finally he came to her during a storm, She saw his ship wrecked near shore.

"Let me come with you now" she whispered.

But she waited for destiny instead.

He survived the wreck but with ill effect and hid and died mysteriously.

Torn with grief at her beloved's defeat, She too succumbed to mysterious death, For her body, with knife placed in hand, later Was found on bloody sand.

Gail Logan

THE STAR

How I wonder what you are as I gaze at you from afar.

Are you just a star or an entire galaxy?

And do you travel away each day or are you getting closer to us.

What message do you convey?

Our data, when implemented with telescopes and images displayed on

Computer screens, perhaps distort the image of what you really seem to be.

Perhaps we should put aside the data and let go of ego and esteem.

Let's bask in your pale light instead, and not

Wonder if you are a stepping stone to other worlds and

Species fortunately living too far away to be on display in a laboratory

some day.

Twinkle, twinkle little star, please hide wherever you are.

Somehow tell us to stop playing the game of environmental roulette.

Let us humbly bow to something greater than ourselves for in doing

So little star, we truly will be looking at you and not our selfish selves.

Gail Logan

THE ORCHID

You are a vision of hope a smile that turns away the evils
That would prey on your woodland dream. You are
An oasis of peace, found in a modern world that doesn't
Fit with the heavenly beauty you bring.
With your delicate pink petals displayed upon a plant hidden along
A trail, your smile is one where the curse of darkness
Will not prevail
Only the fairies may glimpse your true glory though
For you do not toil or spin, and your simple
Orchid beauty and geometric shape,
Symbolize the beauty of a better place,
not the contentious wills and evils of this present space.
Soon your delicate pink petals will fold, and fade. You
Will sleep for another year but the brilliance and hope you
Convey is lasting from day to day.

Gail Logan

THE PARTRIDGE (PERDIX)

Can a bird have a human connection?
Call it what you may but that connection came about
In an unusual way.
For after designing the compass, a great achievement, after all,
Fame came his way when Perdix, nephew to mytholody's
Daedalus, fell into his uncle's company in quite a literal way.
He became the object of Daedalus' envy and as such,
He was destined for a fall.
Daedalus pushed Perdix from Minerva's temple wall,
But since the goddess realized that she too was guilty of
Envy's flaw, when she turned the girl Arachne into a spider,
For weaving superior cloth, she took pity on Perdix,
And in her role as protectress of inventive wits,
She saved Perdix mid air by clothing him in protective plumage.
Perdix was buoyed upward, at least part way.
For to this day, Perdix is content to fly low in protective fields and
Hedges for he is a bird of great charm, humility, and steadfast dignity.

Gail Logan

THE CROWS

The crows that came calling, that once magnificent band,
So joyous and abundant, seem to have dissolved
Like snow on warmest sand.
The image of black feathery plumage, a symbol of crow like wealth,
Like the crow is becoming a shadow of the crows themselves.
For men have preyed upon and thrown away these intelligent creatures as
if they were insignificant participants in life's daily
Play of pageantry and array.
The crows' communal gatherings on branches of oak, pine and birch,
With friends, cackling and swaying in the breeze,
now are reduced to a pitiful two or three.
These awesome creatures, so bold and beautiful to behold,
Fast are becoming a symbol of birds everywhere that oftentimes
Bear the bitter darkness of men's evil souls.
Their beautiful silky feathers, strewn like ashes from a funeral pyre,
Bring a final note of silence to those who watch, love and cry.

Gail Logan

GAIL

THE FABULOUS BLUE CRAB

When bay waters recede at low tide,
And the sun is high in sky, a universe spanning
A half mile foot deep natural sanctuary extends into the bay
Revealing a world of sand, rock, colorful seaweed, and small animals
That come to life that certain time of day.
Their world is a primitive one but they still have their king.
They are ruled by a blue angular looking creature
Endowed with precision, grace and instinct.
As he maneuvers backwards, forwards and sideways,
The blue crab's uncanny ability to change direction instantly,
Displays intelligence, cunning and ingenuity.
If man or beast suddenly invade his domain though,
He'll back away from them with lightning speed then
Quickly disappear by burying himself in sand where he remains unseen.
Yet if he is forced to confront the enemy, he'll menacingly raise his claws
And stand his ground not just for display but to show others that he is
unafraid,
And ready to fight to the death.
For the little blue crab is a brave warrior and valiant foe.
He knows if he is caught by man, he'll be placed in a pot
And cruelly boiled alive or perhaps even fried.
This beautiful awesome creature should be honored for what he is.
He's lived for millions of years prior to the advent of man,
And he should be rewarded for his survival by recognizing his dignity
and tenacity by heeding nature's plan.

Gail Logan

BOX TURTLE

With yellow and black shell covering his body,
The box turtle is a social little guy, who adapts
To backyards, and makes friends with people providing him
With a bit of food and shelter in their yards.
Yet his ideal retreat is one fast becoming obsolete.
As most of us know the turtle doesn't exactly run and go.
He is slow to get to where he wants to be.
So drivers beware. His prospects of getting to the opposite side
Of the road are slim. So if it's not too dangerous, please pick him up,
and carry him there.
He's probably looking for a new home.
Although he is primarily a land animal, he also likes clean
Water, and like people, he likes to go to the beach.
He'll bask on a favorite rock by a pond until a raccoon or another predator
Takes stock of him and he'll dive into the water, and hide for a short
Time until the predator is gone.
He then might venture into woods, or another natural space.
You see, turtles like people want a place they can call their own.
So please help him out so he can live life in his own home.

Gail Logan

DEAR MOON

I look for you during morning hours when night has slipped away.
You hover over pale moon flowers where dew drops fall from sky until the
Sun pierces the night fairy's haven and she dies.
In the evening, your world again revives. The murmuring of night
visitors, the
Calls of owls, and the whispering of trees swaying in the breeze, begin the
ritual
Of night where fairies, mice, toads and elves dance in a harmonious circle
before your sight.
All things grow and thrive beneath your tidal rhythm and flow. Your pale
veil of
Light honors us with your presence at night, whether it is in a distant
dream or
The delicate beating of bats' wings spread outwardly and touching
moonbeams.

Gail Logan

TRAVEL WITH EASE

No need to travel by plane or train for beauty and nature
Always can be seen at any time when one opens the heart
To the spectacle of creation's great scene where colorful wildflowers
or morning dewdrops on a leaf create a backdrop
for a dreamlike memory of a distant scene:
An endless beach where waves, never ceasing, curl then crash on
A rugged or sandy shore might be accompanied by something more.
The memory of a concerto or symphony orchestra playing in your head
is all that you need to focus on your dream scene ahead.
Just close your eyes and listen to the beautiful world within.
Gather all those beautiful memories and dreams into a bouquet, and
Keep them with you every God given day.

Gail Logan

COTTONTAIL BUNNY

The Easter bunny came in an unexpected way
When a little brown bundle of fur hiding in the grass,
Crossed my path one day.
So delicate was he that he could have been china or glass.

His searching eyes almost made one cry,
And his gentle demeanor seemed to say it all.
"Mother is gone, and I've looked for her but she's not around."
He must be something an angel dropped off at the forest door to be found.
I dared not explore his situation anymore.

The forest was blessed that early Easter morn,
For this little rabbit was truly a harbinger.
He seemed to say that spring is a time for renewal and growth,
And his mother left him there as if she'd left that note.

Care was taken that day to insure his safety, for no doubt
He expected his mother to return for him later, and she did.
He nibbled at a few greens.
He didn't seem at all afraid.
He truly was a special visitor that day.
He came for just a short time to remind us that nature is
Beautiful and sublime, not just for rabbits but for all creatures
That try to live and thrive during these
Earth changing times.

Gail Logan

THE EVENING FLIGHT

A garden comes alive at night when toads, elves and fairies
Delight in dim starlight.
An owl then awakes, shakes off the slumber of day, and withdraws
From a world of man's decadent disarray.
He enters a world,
Where night flowers, flourish and bloom,
Indifferent to daytime's mood.
A huge evening moth lights on a golden pear tree, and silently rests
His wings as a white bat follows, lingering above this garden path where moon
Flowers bloom profusely in all directions, creating a world of near perfection.
The moon emerges from behind a cloud casting pale light on the evening shroud
as the sky fills with the sound of singing crickets, and
The whispering wind harmonizes with the beauty of night
Wooing the mystery of the owl's flight in this region out of sight

Gail Logan

FAR AWAY NEAR A SECRET BAY

There is a bay where polar bears adrift on ice floes,
come ashore and discover a world of
a different mold.
They return to a land they once knew but a place men
Never may know or pursue.
There is no climate change here, and nothing to fear.
For this secret bay has left the modern world behind,
And is self sufficient all the time.
The spirits of reindeer, seals, walruses, sea birds and such
Move within this icy clutch of arctic flowers where once
A melting glacier occupied the place where now
Spring fed waters flow into icy gardens full of snow.
They nourish the inhabitants of this graceful space
Where no violence lurks in shadow near the ponds and,
Animal mothers may raise their young without fear.
Snow gently falls from sky sending
A benign message to polar bears keeping even rhythmic
time in this place,
where ice fairies sip melting snow drops from emerging
Flowers and grass as if this gentle environment was made entirely
Of glass.

Gail Logan

MYSTERIOUS DOMAIN

Caves are mysterious places, and some lying beneath Earth,
are so remote and deep, that their fabled interiors are too difficult
to reach.

Exquisite cave crystals of myriad colors, hues and design,
Form strange patterns when exposed to light, and
Radiate this world out of sight.

Yet such beauty only beckons the fool to enter in.
Narrow, secret cave passageways
Shield minute living and non living things
From a manmade world of sin.

Humans who enter this world might never see light again but always
Remain within sight of eternal captivating beauty of night.

Only a white ghost bat resides inside the cave but
he leaves this secretive place of beauty at night in search
Of insect sustenance flickering around house lights.

As sole animal occupant of this lost cave domain,
His tiny white wings beat so fast he is illusive and quite
Difficult to view over the subterranean world of which he rules.

Gail Logan

MERMAID

She was a mermaid, a vision of the past, when he first saw
Her image in a glass.
So captivated was he at what he seemed to
See, he was determined to welcome her to his reality.
half animal, half divine, this protean like being
could change his image at any time.
He knew what it was like to be a shark, whale or even human,
All at the same time, and he immediately changed into a being appearing
Quite sublime.

She smiled a greeting to the one who wished to bring her to life.
Her hair, long, golden and lovely fell to her waist and she wondered
What it would be like to be held in a god's embrace.

The sea god knew her thoughts for like sharks, whales and porpoises
He sensed another's emotions so he was sympathetic with her lot.

Her long hair streamed out from behind as she followed him below to the
depths
Of the sea, and within that world of colorful coral, magnificent pearls and
Golden seaweed she wed this god so divine.

"I know what it is like to be both animal and human" she told him as she expressed her emotions beneath sea. "The human world never will survive unless men appreciate souls unlike themselves, and cease to capture, destroy, enslave or eat other beings but never let them be free."

"We must replace that image we see of man's decadence," he said holding up a glass in hand. "We must envision another world for men. They must learn to mend their world and blend with the animal kingdom we know or else mankind's peace might never be known, and men may never be whole."

Gail Logan

GAIL

CLOUD FROM ABOVE

Pink blossom cloud fallen from above,
Leads one to a place where there is only heavenly love.
Beautiful, delicate and divine, miniature tiny roseate buds are
The ephemeral essence of soft scented purity and fragrance undefined.
Only sunshine, spilling all around, and yellow butterflies touch this sacred
Oasis and rebuke the sins of men who would crush such heavenly perfection
Without even an apologetic thought or amends.
For such beauty is in contrast to man's sweeping disregard of
The Creator's design, and this heavenly beauty and array.
could be replaced with man's own destructive
Plans and decay.
Nature's diminutive, innocent beauty alone
stands in the way of selfish power underway,
and must be protected and saved everyday.

Gail Logan

ROSCOE

Roscoe languishes in his cage and wonders what the world
Outside is like each day.
His distant memories of the past: a mother's love, rugged bush
And dense green, grassland, hold Roscoe in their grasp today.
As he strains to see outside, he presses his face and nose against
The cold cage bars and cries.

Tears run down Roscoe's snout, as an odd looking little gray haired man,
A circus magician by profession, notices Roscoe's plight, and
Decides to take the lion back in time to a place that defines a better world
For captive lions left behind.

"Calm down, my friend," he says as the lion continues to sob. "My circus
Work is not yet finished here tonight. I am ready to take you home on
A wonderful flight".

Roscoe seemed skeptical of the promising words the magicians spoke.
He had no way to protest but if someone could remove him
From his earthly manmade hell Roscoe silently said, "Just go ahead."

In an instant, Roscoe was free, and reunited with his mother and
other lions, just like life used to be.
The old magician watched the happy reunion with a smile and knowing
Grin and thought, "life in a circus where there are bars, is contrary to
Everything one ever will know about life here on Mars."

Gail Logan

85

DEER FRIENDS

Each day two deer brothers hide amidst darkened forests.
They wait until light of day lifts night's heaviness so they may
Search for a legendary herd wandering hidden terrain.
Neither ancient arrow nor mortal weapon deters this ghostly band
And the band comes and goes at its own command.

Ever since mother deer left them,
to search for a spring that
Bubbles up clear and pure, the brothers look for her amidst
A forest clearing where they first saw her disappear.

They pass the sacred spring where pure waters gush,
And they search for mother's path and find a track where first they
Thought she was lost.

Yet it was not until past sunset and near twilight when the call of forest
night birds
Permeated the air, that the sound of a rustling breeze
awakened their senses to something strange and never before seen.
Mother deer stood amidst the ghostly herd as the brothers
Half trembling in fear and glee, took their places beside her
where a ghostly light revealed a forest bright, and a world
embraced by Nature's brilliant heavenly light.

Gail Logan

NATASHA

Sometimes Natasha's image appears in the clouds above
For she leads the way across sky whenever
She isn't grazing at an elephant sanctuary field nearby
Or wallowing in a forest pond or watching a wonderful day unfold.
So different is she from other elephants you see.
For Natasha is not just a retired circus elephant, she is a star,
And by far the most glamorous elephant of all time for she is on par
With the great Houdini and other artists who engage in the dangerous,
breathtaking and sublime.
She doesn't brag about her life's accomplishments though, such as the time
she led an expedition across the Cloud Bridge in the sky which is
No small achievement for anyone who doesn't understand gravity or how
Difficult levitation can be, especially for an elephant that weighs alot, you see.
Yet Natasha isn't satisfied to remain where she is in life.
Thanks to an elderly circus magician she knows and a
Few other human friends who are as bold as she, Natasha has learned to
travel through time with ease.
She regrets, when she travels, of having to leave a few friends behind
But she is happy and aglow when she returns to them, and realizes that
They still miss her even though she is gone most of the time.

Gail Logan

Poet, Gail Logan would like to point out that Natasha the elephant is a major character in two of her three trilogy novels,

Natasha continued

Natasha the elephant is sometimes seen in the clouds for she
Moves with the wind and crosses a cloud bridge at whim.
Although she once weighed nearly a ton,
She's been transformed from a circus elephant that
Came to life again after her real image
Somehow was erased from a computer screen.
But since elephants like Natasha never give up hope
Of being reincarnated someday,
She is back alive and full of joy as she trumpets happily in the sky.
So do as Natasha does and hold on to hope and
Always remember to love,
Not just yourself but others as well.
And please don't forget animals because
They seem to need it the most these days.
Yes, Natasha is a dream elephant in many ways,
She even found her way into a book I wrote one day.
For her kindness is found not just in clouds above
But in all the things we know and love.

Gail Logan

DEAR MOON, PART TWO

Tonight your pale moon face shines amidst world strife.
Like some bright image of hope, your gentle light invites men to recognize
Your presence as being an extraordinary sight.
Today only nature's creatures have heeded your call.
For men are isolated from you, and often
They hide behind their electronic devices, and don't see your wonder at all.

Tonight a lazy long haired feline escapes from her human home.
She joins in the magic, and like some ghostly image, she dances and turns
Beneath you sight, and alerts deer hiding in brush that hunting season is
over tonight.
The raccoon and silver opossum already are on hand.
They join in the celebration as if they were listening to a celestial one
moon band.

The barn owl in flight forgets his tasty morsel tonight, and the field mouse
Below finds her snug shelter shielded by crunchy snow.
For a few exquisite hours, the modern world is forgotten.
Like a blanket of tranquility surrounding them, nature's primeval world is
Preeminent as a gentle warm wind signals the return of spring, and snow
flowers
Emerge from earth, and punctuate the dark wintry scene as a coyote howls,
And your pale moon face smiles down on everything.

Gail Logan

ELEPHANTS OUT OF WORK

With no ticket to perform before circus audiences these days,
Elephants aren't sure if they are welcome to play and to stay.
Poachers hide behind every bush it seems,
And make it too dangerous for elephants even to sneeze.
Living in the rough is tough especially if an elephant has tusks.
Circus life had its drawbacks, but it was fun and the illegal ivory trade
Doesn't help elephants to smile or sleep these days.
Elephants know they have to survive on their own
But how are they to do that when they don't even have cell phones?

Gail Logan

TRIBUTE TO AN ARTIST
WHOSE WORK IS IMMORTAL

Rain like angels' tears falls to ground
Until the sun once obscured by grief emerges
From clouds and eternal beauty lives again
Captured by one whose art is found in
The the myriad hues of blue and gold,
Like some angel visitant from beyond,
The artist's hand reveals creation's smile,
And his paintings forever touch the souls
Of those who understand the brilliant mode
he left behind.

Gail Logan

MISS SWEET DIVA

She gently nuzzled her trainer's hand and
Ate the sugars cubes offered her one at a time.
Why must you race today he wanted to say?
They both knew she couldn't stay.
This beautiful wildflower couldn't run away.
She longed to be surrounded by aromas of
Sweet pasture grass, herbs and hay.
Yet this magnificent creature,
Of enormous courage and might, would stay in the fight.
Hooves pounded turf as the crowd thunderously roared,
And she emerged with the horses she wanted to leave behind.
But suddenly angel wings held her back.
As she raced for the finish line,
They lifted her aloft above the race track,
And she fell realizing she would take another lead today.
She joyfully ran from the turbulent noisy fairground scene and she
Entered a pasture of infinite promise and dreams.

Gail Logan

CAMPAIGN KITTY

Campaign Kitty finds election headquarters inviting.
She hides beneath a worker's desk
And dreams of Morris' Congressional knighting.
He is a national favorite among the furry set,
And not just among fun loving jet set pets.
If only she too had the celebrity to become cat of the hour.
She would do great things.
She gazes at Morris' portrait pasted across a can of filleted tuna.
Campaign Kitty tries to forget the human political agenda.
She embraces the unopened can of Morris' favorite kitty brand:
"four legged friends must be heard," she thinks,
As a worker opens a can of tuna for her.
"Even though man's political agenda is one of awe, it has flaws.
National kitty polls show Morris ahead but I could do better",
She meows.
Then with a consenting paw, she puts the half eaten tuna aside.
She jumps upon a human candidate's campaign table and meows
As if to say,
"Tell the human majority:
There will be no more overcrowded shelters, death sentences for pets,
Or relegation to places where life is quite unfit and unrefined for animals of
Any kind."

Gail Logan

PATHWAY TO HARMONY

White wings spread across sky as
Fantastic herds of majestic horses race to outdistance time,
And leave a man-made civilization in decline.
For men have abandoned the sublime and left it behind.
Like the white doves accompanying them,
The winged horses evade man's war birds falling to the ground.
But hover above a passageway unknown to men and
Guide an animal kingdom toward a hidden glen,
Where the lost paradise of an animal kingdom begins to appear,
And countless animal and bird species
Have nothing to fear.
For freedom is with them at last, and
The vision of Nature's perfection now is clear
As men shrink from the scene and move in their separate ignominious
dream.

Gail Logan

THE BUMBLEBEE COMES

Yellow and striped fuzz ball with a buzz,
Bounces effortlessly amidst the foxgloves.
Alighting with a gentle thud on a red azeala bud
Or on a daffodil bloom with a quick downward zoom,
This diligent bee never greets the day with gloom.
He is too busy earning his keep
To make room for defeat.
Armed with invisible buckets strapped to spindly black
Shiny legs, he collects
All the sweet nectar that hasn't slipped or fallen away
From Nature's bounteous room of colorful blooms.
Each year he jostles Spring awake
So she won't sleep incessantly as if she'd made time her escape.
This year, I fear the bumblebee had to work
Overtime, as with aerodynamic defiance, he pushed frost away
Until Winter became Spring,
And each dawning hour another day.

Gail Logan

GODDESS OF LIGHT
AND DREAMS

Morning glory meets sky and first light touches shadow
When one discovers a moonbeam left over from an evening dream.
Night's face then fades from view and
Becomes at one with morning dew
Where a black and white feline goddess
Divides time between the pastoral and divine.
Instead of hanging from the pale waxing crescent of the moon, you see
Bastet hides behind the trunk of a moss covered tree.
She searches for prey amidst enchanted moonflowers and leaves
But moves from the scene as if she has had enough it seems.
She wanders away amidst fields flooded with sunshine and peace,
Where there is no need to hunt or even look for a treat.

Gail Logan

This poem is written in honor of all the beloved kitties I've known and
still know.

THE WHITE HERON

At the edge of marsh grass,
Bridging the gap between water and land she stands,
Constant yet vulnerable, as she patiently awaits her daily fare
Of minnows and small frogs, to feed herself and young so rare.
Statuesque with long legs and beak,
She is an image of rare beauty and feathery white physique.
Intermittently she emerges from shadow and safety of water's edge
Only to disappear again beneath shelter of mossy ledge.
She shrinks from a changing world
That divides itself into civilized and untamed.
Part of her remains in sunlight, with
Feathers glowing. The rest of her is submerged in shadow,
Her image captured momentarily
On the smooth surface of the lake
Before she quickly moves away again
And disappears like a melting snowflake.

Gail Logan

A MEETING OF FRIENDS

The crows come calling on a cold winter's day
When the sun is falling
But still holds onto its bright rays.
Glossy darkness of sleek feathery coats,
Reflects daylight's brightness as the crows settle peacefully
On branches of wild maple, pine and oak.
Content to be alone like some extended nation of friends,
The crows cackle joyfully not wanting the visit to end.
Such a social gathering is not always a common sight.
Surely there must be at least fifty of these feathery fellows
Here this early December night.
The sun is slowly sinking but the crows will not be gone.
They stay gathered together expecting the sun
To join their communal bond.
But night is gradually gaining on the glorious sunset waning.
Soon this group of many will fade into inky night.
The rest will then depart, enveloped by winter's slowly
Moving flight.

Gail Logan

THE NIGHT THE CIRCUS LIGHTS DIMMED

She was friend and trainer to a circus elephant,
This girl with a dream but one day she and the elephant
Abandoned the arena with an elderly circus magician it seems.
The old man began his light show routinely but something went amiss.
He opened a gateway to a place that men thought they had erased.
In the distance a strange realm as if in myth reared ahead in mist.
The show was fantastic but the audience suddenly disappeared.
Where was this mysterious place shrouded in rainbow hue?
Natasha the elephant trumpeted triumphantly
As if she knew where they were and where they were going too.
But the magician and the girl found themselves confused
In this primitive land serene,
Where men were unknown and elephants reigned supreme.

Gail Logan

TIGER

Tiger went away one day but he comes to me in such a way,
I seem to see him everyday:
One yellow eye and one brown one peeking at me
Through the corners of my life,
A kinky tail held straight up as he strains to see me
Pulling weeds from my garden or
Placing clothes on the line on a warm summer day,
Sniffing the ground for any food the other cats may have missed,
Digging his claws into the hard red clay,
Or rolling on the ground in bliss; tiger's nine lives
Seem lost in a labyrinth of mischief and delight.
Captured unaware by human hands,
I stroke his yellow striped fur and he purrs relentlessly.
Left on his own at night, tiger joins felines in flight.
They play ball with the moon and howl mercilessly until my beloved
Tabby falls exhausted with them to the ground in sleep.
He then defies the law of gravity
By stealthily climbing to my roof
Top high, where in the morning he descends
To the ground in one leap,
And I find him gazing up at me as if to say,
What is to eat? And of course, I always make sure he has a feast.

Gail Logan

CHEETAH

Swift and illusive gold and black spotted phantom cat,
Hides in tall grass.
Stealthily she wanders deep into the African plain,
Until she makes a kill that will feed her family today.
An exhausted mother cheetah then
Gazes into the distance before retreating into a tree where she
Rests in branches hidden by leaves.
She knows just enough food and water is needed for survival
But finding such daily sustenance is a daily battle.
Her young patiently await mother cheetah's arrival home,
They remain still and calm for such behavior is essential for survival.
Cautiously mother cheetah returns with food,
And with relief, her family greet her.
They are frightened when she leaves them.
They know mother doesn't like to hunt but at
least they will eat today, and they are grateful for the prey.
Cheetah rapidly is disappearing from the African stage.
For man like a deadly cobra, continues his conquest of the plain, and
His relentless growth and expansion
Forces Cheetah and other animals into darkest night and pain.

Gail Logan

Gail

ANGUS

Angus is ponderous. That's why he has wanderlust.
He gazes beyond the pasture fence and realizes there is a world
Beyond the one he has come to sense.
He gratefully moos as he discovers a fence hole beside a trodden path,
Where he makes his escape and discovers freedom at last.
Today he visits an astounding lake where he pauses to take a break.
The summer air is warm, the water cool and comforting.
Angus wades into waters deep and plucks a lily bloom from off a leaf.
He swims ashore, stops to gaze at birds in trees,
Then brushes a bee away as he discovers a field of flowery array.
Some buds are yellow, others purple, pink or blue.
He sniffs then munches a bunch then savors the tender flavor of such
A delicious lunch.
Angus isn't on a fast track; he never regrets what time lacks.
He has found his own pace you see, for he moves in timeless reverie.
He glances upward as the day begins to slacken.
The sun is lower in the sky. Perhaps he should
Return to a barnful of friends that will want to know
What life is like on the other end.
On his way home, Angus will pay me a visit.
He'll stand at the end of my driveway, and gaze at me as if to say, "It's good
to see you. I want you to know, I'm free today as all animals should be."

Gail Logan

Gail

ANGUS REMEMBERED

His legacy became apparent when he escaped the pasture,
And merged with the woodland scene.
His huge hoof prints aren't here today.
His signature remains and will be forever conveyed.
He is a sign of the Zodiac: A bull written in the stars.
It is hard to define one so fine as Angus the divine.
Whenever the birds sang a soulful tune,
Angus inwardly sang with them, melodies profound and true.
He caught life's easy rhythmic beat and rarely caved into defeat.
Even if friends disappeared from the pasture, Angus didn't mourn them.
He sang them a song of joy and rapture.
He was a connoisseur of the Earth, a bull that loved Nature's gifts:
Especially flowers that sent their precious fragrance his way,
Or the butterflies that landed on his nose in play.
One day he left them all when he wandered away through a sunlit haze.
I shall search the heavens for Angus tonight.
He has moved from this world's encroaching cruelty and strife.
He is an observer from afar.
He is Taurus the Bull, a sign of hope in the stars.

Gail Logan

THE VISITING BEAR

The visiting black bear braves his days alone.
His tracks are small and aren't mother bear's at all.
Dogs grow restless as from afar they hear a bear's lonely cry.
He whines not out of mischief or fear.
He cries because he is hungry,
And hopes mother soon will appear.
He wanders down to the old marsh ground where frogs, turtles
And snails abound.
Mother has taught him how to find
A morsel or two but he is unhappy
The turtles quickly dive into the pond on cue.
Surely this woodland visitor to our forest ground
Will not stay long after mother bear comes around.
Instead they will disappear into a rainbow haze,
Where they will fish in a crystal pool by an endless cave,
And live without fear or need each perfect day.

Gail Logan

FOREST MUSIC

The woodlands are alive this day.
The distant freeway traffic
is muffled by pelting clatter.
Squirrels and other small animals,
So visible to the daily scene, suddenly
Scatter to find shelter amidst the leafy trees.
Yes, the forest bells are ringing
With all their magical singing.
The raindrops, like tiny bells,
Have gathered upon the ground.
They form little puddles
Where toads have come around.
They enjoy this perfect weather, and
Join the elves and fairies who
Dance upon a fallen feather,
Swap tales of long ago,
Or dance a ring around a tree
Where a spider spins a web within the gentle breeze.
Yes, the rain that falls upon the spider's web
Is caught like crystal drops but
Summer sun soon intrudes upon the spot, and
Forest bells stop ringing,
The birds resume their singing and
The light of day with its delicate rays,
Touches earth with its welcoming mirth,
Enfolding each living thing
Within a colorful rainbow scene revealing
All to be an integral part
Of Nature's daily dream.

Gail Logan

THE SEA TALES OF LONG AGO

The ancient tales of those who remember the ships of long ago,
Will tell you of a time known as Mid Summer's Eve, when wrecked ships
Give up their secrets to those who watch and see.
On this night, movement of light and shadow beneath a half moon and
glassy sea,
is watched from a lonely beach by those who remember with grieving
hearts that
ancient ships once broke apart near here in heavy seas.
Tonight along this silent coast if you will believe, you might see ghostly
Ships rising from an ocean floor, and bearing
the image of ships once new, whole and free;
They rise from the sea's depths to tell the tale of a journey and phantom
Destiny.
Some were lost or sank during spring storms of long ago.
And one ship rode a tidal wave,
And came ashore in a Cape Cod meadow, where tonight its
Bones visibly rise from the soil as if they rose from sea.
Legendary ships of the past remain lost and abandoned only to
Those who won't believe that they still sail;
The greatness of these ghost ships remains undiminished.
For these ships still thrive in the soulful majesty and mystery
Of the sea, and in the hearts of those remembering that these ships once
Plowed through rough oceans and brutal weather before becoming victims
tethered to the sea's cruel and baffling tales of forever.

Gail Logan

*Some of the ghost ships referred to here are, The Jason, The Sparrowhawk,
The Eagleflight, The Commodore Hull and The Whydah, to name a few.

THE DEER KING

In the middle of the highway he stood:
A king, statuesque, his antlers a crown;
An anachronism, a figure enshrouded by darkness.
He was ready to die in the path of oncoming cars:
Cars driven by self absorbed people who didn't see him.

Hands squeezed the car's steering wheel,
A foot hit the brake pedal.
Cars behind one another swayed and slowed down.
A car was on the road's shoulder:
Inside the car was a person with head bowed,
Relieved the moment had passed without incident.

The deer king had crossed the road.
He disappeared into the right until death finds him
In the path of progress and self-destruction.

Gail Logan

THE METEOR

How beautiful you are this starry night.
You arch across sky like some herald of light.
Beneath you, the world lies silent and still.
Only a coyote witnesses your fall so near.
He howls triumphantly at Nature's grand profundity.
This meteoric symbol of universal power touching all things great and
small,
Seems like a brilliant sign binding all things together
In some heavenly endeavor.
The shabby frail coyote momentarily is bathed in light
As a hand mightier than man's guides this falling star over land
Where wasteful destruction momentarily is eclipsed,
And a brilliant symbol of hope amidst
Dismay leads the world forward above
Wanton discord and decay.

Gail Logan

POLAR BEAR DREAMS

Large polar bear tracks cross my mind in icy dreams of a better time.
Glacier filled lakes stretch for miles
Across a wide ghostly sea where the polar bear wanders free.
Nothing thwarts him in this distant place.
Life goes on at a steady but endless pace where thousands
Of birds, seals and such things, live out their lives as Nature intended it to be.
There are no fences here and nothing to fear.
No harpoon's deadly dart, nothing to tear the polar bear's world apart.
Each day is spent as it should be wallowing beneath the
Cold arctic sun or fishing for abundant food until the day is done.
As I gaze from my window this cold wintry day, I envision the
Ancient polar bears at play.
Like a valiant army, they've come to roll back time.
They march along one at a time across an icy land bridge;
Their harmonious rhythm has created a new beat.
They've set foot on this present Earth not as prisoners of a deadly clime
But as harbingers.
They've come not to die or to give into defeat.
They've come to warn us that we mustn't compete
With Nature's steady natural beat. We must keep in step with their
Distant day or lose our footing entirely and become slaves
To a selfish and inferior man dominated age.

Gail Logan

MAMA KITTY

My home is a haven to many a critter.
They've come to stay and won't be quitters.
Mama, my white fluffy tabby cat, is distant and invincible.
She rules my front porch and steps as a matter of principle.
She hisses at Leo the chow if he invades her domain.
She bares her claws fiercely until Leo obeys.
Like some giant hairball, Leo turns to leave.
He eyes Mama's food bowl first to see if there is anything
Good left to eat.
Mice and birds in shelter of nearby bushes,
Scurry away if Mama approaches.
Birds in a nearby birdbath keep a watchful gaze
On Mama's innocent feline play.
At night, when Mama dances beneath the moon,
Marauding raiders arrive in hope of stealing food;
An opossum climbs a nearby tree.
He knocks the bird feeder down so he may eat the sunflower seeds.
A scavenger raccoon joins in the fun until Mama appears.
She has come to make them silently obey her.
With a whisk of her tail, she conveys a message.
Night is waning. It's time for nocturnal visitors to leave.
Like some conquering queen from a distant past,
Mama leaps upon porch steps,
Then with her mesmeric eyes so tender,
Mama bids the sun to rise anew so she alone may bask in its splendor.

Gail Logan

THE GHOST SHIP JASON

On a still midsummer night, under half moon and pale moonlight,
The ghost ship Jason, rises from calm sea.
Guided by a phantom crew, steering this ship aloft, the Jason
Sails slightly into the sky before descending and resting upon
Sea and sand bar.
Like some kind of night bird, the phantom ship then rises;
Gliding slightly above
Foam crested waves that glisten and crash upon a bar.
Rising even higher above waves and again into sky,
the ship then rests beneath the pale ghostly half moon
As the eerie sound of surf below breaks upon an endless lonely beach
And sea music resonates softly, touching the heavens above,
while the ship continues to sail aloft.
When the moon disappears amidst darkening cloudy sky
The Jason finally descends, and
At early sunrise and dawn, comes to rest on ocean floor
Before rising, and sailing upon an unseen ocean far from shore.

Gail Logan

THE DUCK AND GEESE NEIGHBORS

How secretive you are.
You guard your little families hidden amidst the high weeds;
Wary of intruders who might interfere
With your best laid plans for the year.
You hiss, quack and quake
But dare not escape if an intruder unaware encroaches upon your nests.
This is your home and space, a place to rest.
Shared by your families of duck and geese,
You hover over your nests with all the diligence
Concentration attests.
You are community: Families working together.
You fool those who might be so cruel
As to interfere or destroy your sphere.
You are meek and contrite but
Determined if taunted to put up a fight.
Even the raccoon in flight hesitates to approach your space
And steal one of your tasty eggs in sight.
If only men were as content to live as close to the land
As this feathery band,
There might be peace everywhere.
Friends as brothers would live alongside one another
And make the best of this
World's fast moving pace and dwindling wilderness space.

Gail Logan

EARTH'S FRAGILE CORRIDOR

Last spring's bluebird has left her nest,
And the yearly sojourn between each quest, is longer and without rest.
The glassy pond is nearly frozen but a late standing heron's
Reflection in it, acknowledges the silent and unspoken.
The scene has shifted and in its wake, an invisible door has opened a
corridor leading
To a fantastic winter scene where melting glaciers and weeping icicles
Convey the images of a dying wintry dream.
The mighty polar bear has but disappeared from our age,
And images of walruses, seals and penguins are melting away
As if they too are evaporating today.
Are we fools to be deceived by what we don't perceive?
These magnificent beings of another age are being enfolded by another
time, and unknown clime, and tonight's aurora borealis is wrapping them
in the eternal and Divine.
Gail Logan

GHOSTLY VOICES OF GRISWOLDVILLE

A ghostly melody creates a somber song
That permeates nature's voices when the day is young and long.
At first you think you are dreaming of this melody so intriguing.
As you move immersed in sunlight brilliance,
The song persists to haunt you like something come to encompass you.
Voices seem to come from directions near and far.
They repeat a melody suggesting a strange hypnotic bar.
Music lost in rhythm is like the sound of someone trudging along.
The muted notes of a distant bugle call,
The muffled sound of drums, are heard once and then again,
As if the song should never end.
The voices finally grow faint and fade.
But the melody has been conveyed.
A battle once was fought here upon this sacred ground.
And the melody, the ghostly melody and intense early morning light,
Linger, remembering those who walked here,
Who stood their ground and continued to fight.

Gail Logan

PHANTOM HORSES

She ran away one summer,
A distant time ago'
I knew I couldn't follow;
I had to let her go.
They moved like lightening over a pasture fence.
"Oh no", I thought, "Misty is gone again".
They played and danced frenetically beneath a threatening sky.
I held my breath and prayed.
Perhaps death could be defied.

They leaped across a canyon wall,
And sailed into the sky.
The phantom kept her with him until she fell and died.
He went to her. He nudged her gently until she woke anew.
She rose again, and then they danced amidst the purple hue.

Many years have passed now.
I never shall forget,
The fateful night he called to her
When she quickly ran and left.
Sometimes when it's silent and the midnight sky dark blue,
I see them prancing and dancing beneath
The fullest moon.
They seem so very blissful.
I know they've finally won.
They've found their love together.
Death has been overcome.

Gail Logan

SCRUFFY

A traveler by the roadside playing in a country stream,
Scruffy was skin and bones,
And seemed to have great need.
His brindle coat all wet revealed
A slight bony form so very small.
He followed me down the road
Until I stopped as if he'd called.
I knew he needed a home,
A place where he would be protected.
Scruffy needed love for he had been rejected.
I scooped him up in my arms.
His warm little tongue licked my face.
Today Scruffy has found more than a home.
He has found a place.
His pointed terrier ears, and alert little form
Straining at his leash is a reminder of all the things
He does for me and how he earns his keep;
A lost glove retrieved from the ground,
Is sure proof, Scruffy never should be relegated to a pound.
A welcoming bark when coming home
Is something never postponed.
Scruffy does his utmost best to make sure folks never feel alone.
He skips and plays with retriever Lillie Bea,
Who has learned to ignore old age.
Even though we three are quite tethered
He takes us on our walks together.

Two steps at a time, a rapid eager gait.
Scruffy knows how to exercise,
And never lets one be late.
Yes, Scruffy has entered my world in so many delightful ways.
I'm grateful that he is here with me,
And that he has come to stay.

Gail Logan

THE GRATEFUL ROOSTER

It's five A. M., the world is asleep
But red rooster doesn't slumber in the least.
Full of vim, vigor and eager to start the day,
Rooster flies to the nearest line of defense:
A comfortable corner post a few feet from the garden fence.
He hesitates, He stretches his neck as far as it will go,
And then calls out with a mighty crow.
He knows the sun soon will arise
In all the resplendent glory it can advertise.
A brave little feathery soldier, willing to abet the sun's mighty cause,
Rooster stands proud and ready.
Even if the new day has a few flaws,
Rooster will pretend he doesn't know.
If it's about to rain or snow,
He'll still let out with a lusty crow
Or maybe it's just a raspy hello.
Whatever the weather though, Rooster puts on a mighty show.
He always is grateful when he meets each blessed day.
He never hesitates to tell the rest of us
To arise and greet this world with praise.

Gail Logan

THE CAUTIOUS TREE FROG

Like magic, her strong delicate legs
Grip the window pane
Before she jumps and lands miraculously,
One hardly knows where, perhaps
Behind a plant or beneath a garden chair.

Only cautious croaking suggests her fragile existence
Within life's changing framework where
Her primitive call grows silent if men encroach upon her domain.
Like a visitor from an alien world, she is as distinct
And separate a creature as any one might behold deep within Creation's
Unknown fold.

For she hides from those who would alter her world,
And each day she moves farther away from earthly civilization.
She disappears into a different time and day
Away from men who have lost the way.

Gail Logan

TWO MUSES

J.T. and Doc don't inspire they talk.
Life brims with enthusiasm when they're on the spot.
Doc's loquacious whistle punctuates each phrase.
"Hello Mama" he'll say in his cockatiel way.
He hops from cage and flies to the top of the Chinese screen.
I start to write a phrase or two but J.T.'s loud chortle
Says he's got a message too.
He flies from the parakeet cage to a curtain nearly.
He hides then drops to a table top high.
He inspects what I've written with curious eye.
I turn on the computer printer that whirs out a warning;
Birds must retreat.
Admitting defeat, I reach for a box of birdie treats.
My friends devour the box's contents with greed so to speak.
Enough I say putting papers away.
I fly from the room.
It's time to call it a day.

Gail Logan

THE HARMONY OF LIGHT
AND DARKNESS

The night fairy dies but she revives when light kisses darkness
And the sun departs from sky.

It is then that the night fairy's rule becomes supreme
Within that world of mystery and hidden dream.
Night music resonates and forest nymphs dance
To nature's lyrical symphony and evening chants.
A frog chorus permeates marsh grass, and the hoot owl's
Distant call is heard above the feral cat's distant howl

As a light summer breeze moves through trees
In the distance, crickets play their fiddles in a field
Where elves and forest fairies dance and form a ring
Around the moon, enveloping all who believe and perceive
The enchantment of night's endless star filled scene.

Gail Logan

WILD PIG/LOST HABITAT

Wild pig lives in the brush, and
For some his life doesn't mean much.
But to secretive friends like the wood fairy and toad,
The pig defends territory without being told.
His haven lies deep within a shroud of wild jungle
Where diminishing habitat is a concern, and a raven's cry
Often warns frogs and river birds of intruders nearby.
His yard is where a partridge or two finds shelter
Or an abandoned dog left to die, cries under a darkening sky.
Yet hope never wanes in this assembly of friends, and
Life goes on with dignity and without end.
At sunrise as the wood fairy touches wild flowers,
And the Creator's light reveals dewdrops fallen from sky,
The dog finds food a stranger left behind.
Kindness is not erased within this hidden realm;
Its occupants here are lovingly embraced as
Sun light moves across the tops of trees,
And geese, hiding in marsh grass press forward
And bravely ascend into morning's endless dream.

Gail Logan

GRAY WOLF/ETERNAL PACK

Why would I miss you when you've left one place for another?

You aren't far away.

Your memory still blends into Earth's scene.

Yet you, the symbol of nature's wild freedom, shining like a daystar,

Have been taken from the world today.

Death came so suddenly, that Nature alone realizes the sad profundity.

The ground where you bled is covered in red clover.

I vainly look for you and tears fill my eyes.

No longer do you and your offspring romp and play in spring sunshine.

Instead raindrops silently fill sky and fall to ground along a path where wild yellow flowers once grew in midday sun.

A gate opens and you and your brother wolves follow a scent along a trail, where life's pattern ends, and a great abandoned rabbit hole becomes a place of no return where night is day and darkness light,

And reality, never a matter of sight and sound, places all things earthly last. And the infinite arrangement of stars in the heaven, breaks through tiny holes in night's fabric as you enter the light of a new forest home.

Gail Logan

HUMMINGBIRD HIGHWAY

He's not always there when you look behind.
He lives in a place quite hard to find.
You see him for just a second or so:
A glimmer of light hovering above a rose.
You follow him along a path unseen,
Until you enter his reality
Where the soulful sounds of nature
Never are swept away,
And the fragrant flowers of summer
Are there with you all the day.
This garden path of long ago,
Of toads and elves and fairies, you know,
May not be found without some trust
For when the hummingbird discovers you're there,
He'll simply vanish into thin air,
Taking you from his world unseen,
Until you awake with only the memory of a dream

Gail Logan

LUCY AND THE SCHEME OF THINGS

A mother first in everything,
Lucy never would allow her puppies to stray for anything.
A tragedy came about when Lucy's puppies were taken
From her and she was without.
It's as if those adorable teddy bears melted away,
Like thin ice when sun touches frost on a warm wintry day.
Where did Lucy's puppies go?
I'd like to know.
Did they get swept like rain down a storm drain?
I never heard any barking or crying that day.
Where do puppies go when they aren't loved along the way?
Puppies without a place in life must find a home.
An old shoe becomes more than something to chew upon.
It is an entrance to another realm, a dimension bathed in pure light
Where puppies may chew a hole in the shoe and find it leads to a
Tunnel of delight complete with toys and games to play
And family love conveyed each day.
Puppies here are content and at peace, and
Watching them from afar and through a rainbow haze is mother dog.
She realizes her offspring have found a home.
For mathematically speaking everything must fit within the ideal scheme,
And puppy placement is a REALITY and not just a DREAM.

Gail Logan

WHEN THE WOODPECKER COMES

I listen for the woodpecker's haunting call but today,
It's far away, replaced by noise and dismay.
Austere winter encompasses this once sunny land.
All around are bloody clotted hoof prints of stalked
Deer on frozen ground.
If only civilization would go away, and leave this hidden place
Perhaps the woodpecker would come knocking
And silent discord's taunting.
In the early morning hours when the world is deep in sleep,
The din of machinery leveling pine trees' greenery,
is heard by forest residents disturbing restful peace.
The ground squirrel flees in terror, followed by the opossum
Who dares not delay.
The tired old night owl, finally asleep, suddenly awakes and escapes his
Nest in quest of another place to rest.
The hummingbirds scatter amidst the horror of this pattern.
Only the woodpecker's distant haunting call is heard above the woodland
Clatter of it all.
He calls for forest animals to return to eternal spring,
And with preeminence create a new pattern within the
Shatter by replacing beauty for the lost forest's sorry scene.

Gail Logan

MYSTERIOUS VISITOR

Silently you peer into my window.
You are drawn to me and I to you.
You've come from a world I know nothing about.
Now delicate and green, your form changes, ready to take flight.
"Don't go," I whisper brushing a hand against glass.
"Are you real or an ethereal vision from another dimension?"
You hover in mid air as if you understand my thoughts.
"What message do you bear this enchanted summer night?"
You do not answer.
Instead you spread your wings against the window glass
Like some alien lover come to enshroud my soul
In a powerful emotion.
The light of our separate universes has attracted one to the other:
We stand in awe. You seem entranced by the contact.
If Love's light is extinguished you will escape.
You must not be held behind the confines of glass forever.
You must leave.
Your world is lost to the one humans know.
Your wondrous form is beheld one last time.
Butterfly wings spread against glass.
I switch off the light.
You escape into darkness, a messenger from beyond.
A mysterious form lost in flight.

Gail Logan

THE DREAM

Is evil always real or is it illusion to be swallowed up by good, the perfect and sublime?

Perhaps that was the case when Giuseppe Tartini was convinced that he came face to face with the symbol of evil. The period was the early 1700's.

The composer was alone one evening, and listening to the wind in trees and branches that scratched against his window until the wind suddenly subsided. Relieved that the storm had past, the tired, discouraged Giuseppe Tartini, who found himself unable to compose anything lately, sadly extinguished the candle by his bedside, and fell asleep. Strange dreams haunted him and caused him to toss and turn, until he suddenly sat up in bed and saw at the foot of his bed, the devil with bow and violin in hand begin to play a hauntingly beautiful sonata which surpassed anything the composer ever heard before. The unearthly melody took the form of a complicated sublime composition that drew the composer into the intricate series of trills and a melody of surpassing sophistication and beauty. When the music ended at dawn and the devil disappeared, the composer moved first to his harpsichord and then took up his violin as he tried to play, and compose some of the sublime music the devil had so generously played for him without asking from him anything in return.

The portion of The Devil's Trill that the composer produced became the most successful composition the composer ever would create and that music, even though he could only recall a small portion of its unearthly beauty, brought the composer great success.

The Gift of Music
Lyricism beyond compare, is a timeless gift
That flows to earth from an immortal being
Most never will encounter or know.
A fallen angel's music from above

132

Touched a tired composer's soul one night and
Fulfilled his life long goal.
Shadows disappeared in darkest night, and heavenly trills touched
Earth surrounding one
with music that enchanted and thrilled as no other music could.
On such a momentous occasion, evil became no more.
The composer was lifted above his turmoil, pain and discouragement by
music that transformed and inspired
Him to recreate a musical memory of a mystical meeting.

Gail Logan

PATRIARCH OF THE CARDINAL FAMILY AND FEATHERY FRIENDS

He hides in the brush behind a large pine tree,
And for all intents and purposes,
He appears to enjoy his privacy.
Celebrity is one reason the cardinal lives the way he does.
He's shy of people who follow him around too much
Or take his picture especially if it's too close to his nesting space.
Except for easy access to a couple of bird feeders nearby,
The cardinal stays close to home, avoids crowds, and
Flits around near a bird bath in summer
Where he and extended family members
Like to frolic and play alongside chickadees and
Woodpeckers who convey the same style of bird living
The easy bird way.
Although these birds of a feather enjoy their space,
When winter arrives they all seem less sure of the place.
They envy the domesticated parakeets inside a cozy house
Where parakeets don't have to be afraid of
Neighborhood cats since the home owners are bird lovers and
Parakeets can ignore any potential attack.
Yet for bird fellows on the outside that's quite another story.
The cardinals, chickadees and woodpeckers outside chirp and call aloud
Especially if there is a cat nearby or on the prowl-----meow.

Gail Logan

LIVING LIFE HIS OWN WAY

Guiding him across the road
That cold foggy morn was a benevolent hand he didn't see,
A hand that would lift him out of his misery.
The forest he once knew now mostly was gone.
He was confused.
All that he loved had disappeared.
The dim headlights of an unseen car
Bore down on him.
Large, primeval and out of place in this modern world,
This king of the forest, make no mistake, was not king of the road.
The person driving the car didn't care about a mere bear.
A symbol of a disappearing age was in the way, and bang, the bear
Was left lying upon the pavement, and the car went on its way.
Stunned, frightened and now blind, he dragged his 550 pound body
off the road, and in a heap, he fell asleep.
So deep was the sleep that the wandering bear never did awake.
He was taken away by men who didn't
Know how hard he'd tried to hide and survive
In a world that defied all the things he'd tried to live by.

Gail Logan

OH, FOR THE COUNTRY LIFE

Raccoons are wanderers of sorts. Some find city life exhilarating and
They shelter in secret places or forage in trash cans for a meal.
For most animals, such a life isn't exactly a delight.
The food is spoiled and nasty, and the city slicker
Raccoon is too crafty to stay around for such manmade disaster.
After being chased by an alley cat or two, the raccoon is no fool.
He's convinced that his cousins in the country have a better life that he
is due.
So while sitting under a city bridge one smoggy morn, the city raccoon
is reborn.
Undetected he boards a cargo boat headed upstream where
The county life is recommended and respected.
Oh what bliss, thinks our friend as he sniffs around upon arrival.
He proudly joins the ranks of the "survival of the fittest" and then reflects on
The comparison between where he is and where he once lived.
Is this place heaven or is it impending hell he wonders as he recalls
Being thrown off a city bus one cold November night.
Conditions here aren't governed by humans this time.
But when raccoon manages to forage for a tasty meal in the marsh,
His dinner plans are rudely interrupted by a bear in pursuit, and the
survival
Stakes get even higher when a bobcat hiding in a deep forest tree, denies him
Shelter overlooking a free flowing stream.
Can life get any tougher laughs the little raccoon as he tries to cheer
himself up a bit?
He then heads downstream towards the place where the falls split.

Gail Logan

THE TIDE IS FULL

Silver and phosphorous waves glisten in moonlight as she sees his welcoming image.

He gently leads her to the place where dark green seaweed and ancient coral sands

Cover the sea's inhabitants.

The tide is full. Deep waves arise from the sea's black depths, and crash majestically along

The shoreline, where a shell's spiral outline reflects the ceaseless motion of endless tides and currents.

She picks up the shell, and her fingers trace the shell's outline until she feels herself at one with the tides and currents surrounding her.

The distance between past and present has diminished, and she is drawn into a pattern that traces life's eternal movement.

The distance between island and mainland has receded.

She will find her way home for he has taken her hand, and he leads her towards eternal sunrise

Along a beach that bears no footprints.

The wind whispers to them as they walk.

The ceaseless soft wind sings a lonely song as her form gradually becomes at one with the greater Love surrounding them, and she recalls the haunting melody and words to a song she heard long ago. 'Let me be in morning sun that streams across sky. Let me walk eternally with the one I love by the majestic blue seaside."

Gail Logan

THE POET'S COMMENTARY

Life must envelop things greater than one's self. It should transcend the individual human experience, and touch a broader spectrum. The poet's world is one that endeavors to reach outside a limited human environment. Here the poet is separate from that environment for I am that poet, and I know what I am talking about.

She writes about other life forms, and tries to depict their joys, anguish and pain as they struggle to survive in this sad, selfish and often decadent human existence. Her poetry is dedicated mainly to the animal and non human world, but she lays her work at the feet of the great poets of classical antiquity, Homer and Ovid, to name a few.

The ancient classical poets recognized no clear defining line between the human and animal, for the classical gods, often depicted as human, have the super ability to take animal or human form whenever the occasion required them to do so.

In this modern human world, it is unthinkable to believe that men can take the form of a non human form but if we are to survive on this planet, we must humble ourselves enough to realize that we need to love non human beings enough to insure their continued existence, as never before. All things are connected, and a healthy ecosystem requires a balance between man, animals and nature.

While this basic philosophy is an important part of the poetry expressed here, another aspect of it touches on great human love and sacrifice. My poem, The "Pirate and Enchantress", is set against a backdrop of enormous natural beauty. The pirate embraces the love for the enchantress for she embodies all the qualities he loves. She lives by the sea, and like the pirate, she understands its power and beauty. Yet they first meet one another when he sees her standing beneath a blossoming spring apple tree. Their struggle is not with nature but with men.

Like the animals depicted in my poetry, they cannot escape the human turmoil surrounding them. For the violent storm presented in "The Pirate and Enchantress" reflects that turmoil, and destroys their idyllic world.

My other love poems are parodies meant only to make one smile or laugh. I am proud of a song I wrote with composer Tony Burnett. STEPS was recorded as a demo. The music is Tony Burnett's but I wrote the words to this song written in a light hearted bossa nova rhythm.

Gail Logan

FINAL POETIC NOTE

My travels to the S. Pacific, S. America and Mexico didn't exclude other places. I am fortunate to have traveled to Italy and other parts of Europe but since my focus of interest was always art or nature I especially enjoyed Rome and Florence where my cousin, also interested in art, enjoyed the beauty and history of those cities.

A few years later in my life, I enjoyed a trip to St Petersburg, Moscow and the Kremlin. I must say, the art and architecture of these two cities, is truly worth seeing. The Winter Palace (The Hermitage), lives up to being one of the world's finest art Museums, and the Kremlin is a treasure trove of wonderful art treasures, buildings and historic artifacts. I loved my visit to the Summer Palaces the seasonal homes of the Tsars (about 30 miles from St Petersburg).—the Catherine and Alexander Palaces— and a glimpse of the nearby Pushkin Estate where I was charmed to see a flock of geese making themselves at home there on a nearby lake. The geese may have been year round residents of this historic Russian venue, but they were so much like the geese I see in Macon, GA all year round, I felt quite at home.

Mainland China also made it into my travel plans. I was privileged not just to visit Beijing with its Forbidden City, a vast array of buildings and labyrinths which lead you into another time where you glimpse the lives of Chinese Emperors but the nearby Great Wall at Badaling. From Beijing, it was on to Xian to see the 259-210 BC ancient Terra Cotta warriors before traveling to Guilin with its beautiful strange mountain like scenery bordering the Lijiang River. My trip to mainland China ended with a visit to the large but colorful city of Shanghai with its glimpse of British Colonialism or buildings that reflect traditional Chinese architecture, like the "Jade Buddha Temple" contrasting with modern industrial Shanghai with its businesses and skyscrapers.

I certainly enjoyed my travels but for the time being, I am content to be at home where I enjoy being surrounded by my own backyard and all the wonderful birds and animals that visit me each day.

Ode to a Pigeon, part two (see page 24)

What a lonely place a park might be without a few lovely pigeons to, see, visit and feed.
So fine and beautiful they are, especially when viewed in the sky and flying in perfect formation as seen from afar.
The sun catches their plumage as they fly not as many but as one, and precisely move together as the sun embraces this gray band with colorful feathers tinged with shades of white, purple, pink blue amidst the changing hues of climate news

While pigeons commonly are seen near shopping malls or atop buildings, there is nothing common about these noble birds. Their species has lived for thousands of years, always adapting to mankind's rises declines and falls and other snafus.

They even have made it through enemy lines, carrying vital messages to our troops during wartime. The pigeon is as clean as the human environment will allow for aren't men and not pigeons responsible for all the environmental mess, turmoil and grime?

We must give pigeons credit for being the hardy little birds that they are, and make sure that they have enough food, water and shelter so they can survive.

Gail Logan

Words & music
by
Gail Logan & Tony Burnett

"STEPS"

Words & music by Gail Logan & Tony Burnett

Latin Rhythm

There is no peace___ in re-trac - ing past___ steps.

Steps bruise___ love's flow - ers___ They

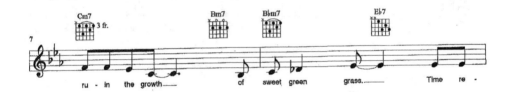

ru - in the growth___ of sweet green grass.___ Time re -

mem - bered should be___ for - got - ten like a road go - in' no -

- where.___ I laugh to e - rase the pain.

I wan-der in cir - cles.

Caught in love's diz - zy - ing path____ I hear your voice____ I

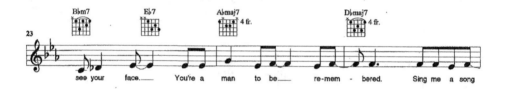

see your face.____ You're a man to be____ re-mem - bered. Sing me a song

____ of wi-ld ros-es in____ the spring.____ Let me taste from your lips____ the

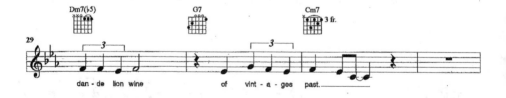

dan - de lion wine of vint - a - ges past.____

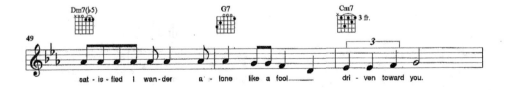

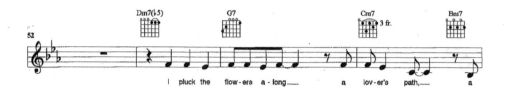

I pluck the flow-ers a - long___ a lov-er's path,___ a

cir - cu - lar path.___ I smell vio-lets of pur - ple twi - light. I wait in

ear - ly ev - 'ning at Love's___ door.

There is no peace in re-trac - ing past steps. I wan-der

back to you___ but love's end-less night is gone.___

STEPS

by Tony Burnett & words by Gail Logan

SINCE WORDS TO SONG APPEAR QUITE SMALL
IN SONG, HERE THEY ARE AGAIN.

There is no peace in retracing past steps
Steps bruise love's flowers
they ruin the growth of sweet green grass.

Time remembered should be forgotten like a road going nowhere.

I laugh to erase the pain
I wander in circles
caught in Love's dizzying path
I hear your voice
I see your face
you're a man to be remembered
sing me a song of wild roses in the spring
let me taste from your lips
the dandelion wine of vintages past
spring is here there are flower everywhere
birds sing to me
the circle I make pushes time aside
love's memory remains, completion found only in retracing past steps
unsatisfied, I wander alone like a fool driven toward
you. I pluck the flowers along a lover's path
I smell violets of purple twilight.

I wait in early evening at love's door
There is no peace in retracing past steps.

I wander back to you but love's endless night is gone.

Footnote: STEPS IS MEANT TO BE SATIRICAL AND EXPRESSES NEITHER THE POET'S EMOTIONS NOR THE SINGER'S EMOTIONS EXPRESSED BY THE SONG.

GAIL

THE END

Printed in the United States
By Bookmasters